ENGLAND'S FORGOTTEN PAST

RICHARD TAMES

ENGLAND'S FORGOTTEN PAST

THE UNSUNG HEROES & HEROINES, VALIANT KINGS, GREAT BATTLES & OTHER GENERALLY OVERLOOKED EPISODES IN OUR NATION'S GLORIOUS HISTORY

with 70 illustrations

Thames & Hudson

First published in the United Kingdom
in 2010 by Thames & Hudson Ltd
181A High Holborn, London WC1V 7QX

First paperback edition published in 2018

England's Forgotten Past © 2010
Thames & Hudson Ltd, London

British Library Cataloguing-in-Publication
Data. A catalogue record for this book is
available from the British Library

ISBN 978-0-500-29377-5

Printed and bound in Glasgow
by MBM Print

To find out about all our publications,
please visit **www.thamesandhudson.com**.
There you can subscribe to our e-newsletter,
browse or download our current catalogue,
and buy any titles that are in print.

CONTENTS

Introduction: Forgetting Ourselves   6

1 — *Making England English*   8

2 — *Lost Landscapes*   34

3 — *Royalty Remembered*   65

4 — *The Blast of War*   84

5 — *Yesterday's Celebrities*   103

6 — *The Inner Man – and Woman*   127

7 — *Believe It or Not*   143

8 — *England Abroad*   163

Sources of Illustrations   186
Sources of Quotations   187
Index   188

✵ FORGETTING OURSELVES ✵

This book is about aspects of England's past that seem to have slipped off the radar of collective memory. Some, like monarchy, the empire, religion and the origins of English identity, are now regarded by many as embarrassing, boring, trivial, marginal or irrelevant. Others, like the history of food or the landscape, have only very recently been recognized as part of 'proper history'.

The inscription on the plinth of the statue of General Havelock in Trafalgar Square proclaims: 'Soldiers! Your labours, your privations, your sufferings and your valour will not be forgotten by a grateful country.' But they have been.

There are a dozen streets in London alone named after Havelock, as well as towns in Ontario and North Carolina, an industrial estate in Singapore, an island in the Indian Ocean, a mid-Victorian hotel in Adelaide, a mine in Swaziland and a seaside village in New Zealand. But could one passer-by in a hundred now say who he was or what he did to merit a memorial at London's very heart?

There is no entry for Tangier in the *Oxford Companion to British History*, yet Charles II spent 20 years and £2,000,000 – about three times what it cost to build St Paul's Cathedral – trying to establish a naval base there. It is as though it never happened.

The entry for the Northumbrian Lindisfarne Gospels in the *Encyclopaedia Britannica* runs to just 56 words – and fails to note that they represent the first example of Christian scripture written in English.

Although England and the English represent the central focus of this book, it treats them both as somewhat permeable notions, fuzzy at the edges. Hoisting his famous signal that 'England expects that every man will do his duty', Nelson must have been aware that only about half the men under his command were actually English.

The empire, like the navy, was British and in both the Scots, Welsh and Irish played prominent, often eminent, parts. However, the values, institutions and lifestyles that empire represented and propagated were predominantly English. Hence the casual way in which throughout the nineteenth and much of the twentieth centuries the terms 'Britain' and 'England' were used interchangeably – much as they are by many people in other countries to this day.

It is a paradox of globalization that it has sharpened the sense of distinctiveness of many national and ethnic groups, with both positive and negative effects, ranging from the vigorous revival of the Welsh language to the brutal break-up of former Yugoslavia. The reactions of the English have been confused. On the one hand, the St George's flag has increasingly come to replace the Union flag on sporting occasions. On the other, a substantial minority still don't know when St George's Day is.

If the English can't remember who they were they run the risk of not knowing who they are. Perhaps a rummage around in the cluttered attic of England's past might be helpful – or, at least, entertaining.

St George has enjoyed widespread and enduring popularity in England since the Middle Ages – this image is taken from a fifteenth-century manuscript – but how did this Roman soldier become so integral to our country's self-image?

1

MAKING ENGLAND
ENGLISH

> *The knowledge of past events…forms a main distinction*
> *between brutes and rational creatures, for brutes…*
> *do not know…about their origins, their race and the*
> *events and happenings in their native lands.*
>
> HENRY OF HUNTINGDON, *HISTORIA ANGLORUM*, c. 1130

Americans have an annual holiday to mark when their nation began. The English have largely forgotten how theirs did. 'English' history conventionally began with the Romans and 'English' kings were named and numbered only from the Norman Conquest onwards.

The period between the Romans and the Normans has pretty much vanished from popular remembrance, largely ignored in the classroom and – with the exception of King Arthur (whoever he was) – apparently of no interest to the makers of movies.

Yet the Anglo-Saxon centuries established the basic institutions that have shaped the nation's life ever since – its language and its laws, its religion and its monarchy. From pennies and parishes to acres and aldermen, the Anglo-Saxon imprint still survives today.

Opposite *Definitely not the Age of Enlightenment: eighteenth-century representations of 'Ancient Britons' as tattooed head-hunters and spear-carrying Amazons.*

MADE BY INVADERS?

Traditionally, school history ignored the 'Ancient Britons', even though they were 'here first'. DNA analysis now implies that they never went away and that a far higher proportion of today's population than was ever imagined may in fact be descended from them.

Successive influxes of Jews, Flemings, Dutch, Huguenots, Italians, Germans and Irish were likewise overlooked. Henrietta Marshall's *Our Island Story* told how England's make-up was produced by successive 'invasions' – Roman, Anglo-Saxon, Viking and Norman. But each was quite different from the others both in its character and its effects.

WHAT'S THIS PLACE CALLED?

The first known account of the British Isles was written by Pytheas of Marseilles, a Greek, in the late fourth century BC. He called its people 'Pritani', probably meaning 'painted people'. Caesar and later Latin authors wrote this as Brittani – hence Britannia for their home and the name of the new province.

THE ROMAN INTERLUDE

The conquest credited to the Roman emperor Claudius in AD 43 was, indeed, a classic invasion – a military expedition for permanent annexation. The Romans swiftly stamped their supremacy with statement architecture – a triumphal arch at their initial base, Richborough, in Kent, and a massive temple honouring Claudius at Colchester, in Essex. Later historians were not impressed. In the words of Suetonius, writing in AD 120:

> *Claudius' sole campaign was of little importance.... He crossed the Channel without incident; and was back in Rome six months later. He had fought no battles and suffered no casualties, but reduced a large part of the island to submission. His triumph was a very splendid one.*

Suetonius appears to be deliberately missing the point. Conquest is about politics, victory is merely the means. Crippled, stammering Claudius, new to the throne and expected to be a puppet, had done what Julius Caesar had failed to – taken over a distant, mysterious island supposedly rich in gold and pearls. And his army must have inflicted casualties even if it suffered few. To be awarded a triumphal procession a commander must have killed at least 5,000 of the enemy – 4,999 wouldn't do.

ROMANIZATION

A Roman frontier was rolled forward to take in what was desirable and defensible – basically England and part of South Wales (the bit with the gold). Scotland was later screened off by Hadrian's Wall. Ireland was ignored.

Veterans were rewarded with confiscated land. A Romanized elite, mostly Gauls, was installed to exploit the land for grain, tin, livestock and slaves, and local luxuries like gold, pearls, oysters and jet.

The historian Tacitus explained how his father-in-law Agricola matched military conquest with cultural subversion:

> *To make a people which was scattered and barbarous, and therefore prone to warfare, grow accustomed to peace...Agricola educated the sons of the chiefs...instead of loathing Latin they became eager to speak it.... Roman dress came into fashion. The next step was towards the temptations of...lounging in arcades, baths and refined dinner-parties. The unsuspecting Britons spoke of such novelties as "civilization", when in fact they were only aspects of their enslavement.*

There was never any thought that 'Britannia' might be Romanized by a mass immigration of Romans. If the local gene pool was diversified it was by intermarriage with soldiers and slaves from homelands as varied and distant as Syria, Egypt, Greece, Nubia, the Low Countries and the Rhineland.

CAMP GOVERNMENT

The Roman occupation was essentially military. It was imposed by the legions and imploded when they left. Enduring place names illustrate the point. Roman legions on the march routinely constructed a fortified camp – 'castra' – every night, destroying it next morning by filling in the defensive ditches with the earth taken from them to build the previous night's ramparts.

Permanent forts frequently became the nuclei of towns. But it wasn't the Romans who went around calling everywhere 'something-caster'. To them Winchester was *Venta Belgarum* – the market of the Belgae tribe. It was the Anglo-Saxon adopted word *ceaster* that indicated a former Roman fort, camp or city – hence Chester, Manchester, Rochester, Dorchester, Winchester, Chichester; but also Lei*cester*, Gloucester, Worcester, Cirencester. In the north of England we find the variants Lan*caster* and Doncaster; and, in the south (and less obviously), Wroxeter and Exeter.

The Anglo-Saxons were also impressed by the Romans' superbly engineered highways and lifted the word 'strata' to mean 'paved road', which became the place name element 'strat', 'stret', 'streat' or '-street' – as in Stratford or Stretford.

So that's you gone then, is it? A fourteenth-century illustrator imagines the departure of the Romans with no concessions to period costume.

When the Romans withdrew their legions after 408–10, the cash economy collapsed, cities were deserted, the fine roads decayed, Latin died out and Christianity, a late implant, withered. The Romans never really Romanized the province they called 'Britannia' beyond leaving it a name for another, greater empire.

> *Legate, I come to you in tears – My cohort ordered home!*
> *I've served in Britain forty years. What should I do in Rome?*
> *Here is my heart, my soul, my mind – the only life I know.*
> *I cannot leave it all behind. Command me not to go!*
>
> RUDYARD KIPLING, *THE ROMAN CENTURION'S SONG*

�֎ FIRST KNIGHT? �֎

No figure on the borderline of history and mythology
has wasted so much of the historian's time.

J. N. L. MYRES, *THE ENGLISH SETTLEMENTS*, 1986

King Arthur probably never existed – but is still heading towards his 1,500th birthday.

MONKISH MEMORIES

The evolution of the legend of Arthur occurred over many years, even centuries. The groundwork was laid when, some time before 547, the monk Gildas, Britain's first known historian, described the arrival of the Anglo-Saxons in a cheery number entitled *Concerning the Fall and Conquest of Britain*. In this he referred to a Saxon defeat at Mons Badonicus – Mount Badon – which stemmed the invaders' advance for half a century.

Then, in about 600, the Welsh war epic *Y Gododdin* backhandedly praised the warrior Gwawrddur as 'no Arthur' – suggesting that the character was already in the collective consciousness. The Welsh monk Nennius, writing in *c.* 830, named an Arthur as 'dux bellorum' (leader of wars), a dozen times victorious over the Saxons, including at Mount Badon.

R. G. Collingwood, an Oxford don, suggested in 1936 that 'Arthur' might have been a freelance commander of Roman-style cavalry who confounded lumbering Saxon infantry with hit-and-run tactics.

HISTORICAL HYPE

Lecturing at Oxford in the 1130s, the inventive Geoffrey of Monmouth raised Arthur to superhero status and embellished his story with the inclusion of treacherous 'Modred', a miraculous sword, mysterious Avalon and a magician, Merlin.

TRACING ARTHUR'S FOOTPRINTS

The appeal of Arthur's legend has scattered England (and in fact the whole of Britain) with locations allegedly linked with the king and his court. The majority of 'Arthurian' sites are, in reality, prehistoric tumuli (Bwrdd Arthur in Wales), henges (King Arthur's Round Table in Cumbria) or hill-forts (Moel Arthur in Wales), which were built centuries before Arthur is supposed to have lived. Several more Arthur-related sites can be found in Celtic-speaking Brittany, the region through which knowledge of the cult first spread to mainland Europe.

ARTHUR'S BRITAIN

Cornwall has Arthur's Bed and Merlin's Rock.

Cumbria has a Stone Arthur. Ancient copper mines at Alderley Edge, Cheshire, are supposed to house the sleeping Arthur and his knights (sadly this tradition dates back only to the nineteenth century).

Wales has three megalithic tombs called Coetan Arthur, two places called Arthur's Stone and King Arthur's Cave.

Near the abandoned Antonine Wall that had once separated Roman Britannia from the Picts stood Arthur's O'en (oven) – first recorded in 1293, it was in fact a ruined Roman building.

Edinburgh is dominated by the spectacularly rocky outcrop known as Arthur's Seat – a long way from where Arthur's capital might have been.

Slaughterbridge over the Rivel Camel in Cornwall is claimed to have been the site of Arthur's last battle, Camlann.

MOUNT BADON

Geoffrey of Monmouth located Mount Badon near Bath, mentioning hot springs. The modern tourist authorities do not go out of their way to contradict him.

The nearest modern name is Badbury, of which there are five, scattered from Dorset to Lincolnshire. The best bet is in Wiltshire, near Swindon, where Liddington Castle recalls a hill-fort guarding a Roman road intersection.

Gildas, writing within living memory of the battle allegedly fought at Mount Badon, described it as at least partly a siege, happening in a populated area with fortifications associated with 'the last of the Romans', whom he called Ambrosius Aurelianus.

GLASTONBURY

Thirteenth-century legend tells us that in AD 63 Joseph of Arimathea came to England with a chalice of Christ's blood and built the first English church at Glastonbury. According to the New Testament it was Joseph of Arimathea who arranged for the burial of the crucified Christ.

The chalice became the Holy Grail of Arthurian legend and was said to have been hidden by Joseph in the Chalice Well, at the foot of Glastonbury Tor, the 500-foot hill standing east of the town.

Glastonbury Thorn, an early variety of hawthorn, said to flower on Christmas Day, is supposed to have leapt out of the earth when Joseph of Arimathea struck the ground at Glastonbury with his staff.

CAMELOT

The location of Arthur's capital has been attributed to the former Roman settlements of Caerleon and Caerwent in Monmouthshire, to Killibury, Camelford and Tintagel

The ghost of Camelot? The hillfort at South Cadbury as depicted in 1719 – by then a matter of antiquarian curiosity rather than national pride.

in Cornwall, to the Iron Age hill-fort at South Cadbury in Somerset, to Winchester in Hampshire, to Colchester (Roman Camulodunum) in Essex and to Almondbury (also Roman Camelodunum) in Yorkshire.

TINTAGEL

Both Geoffrey of Monmouth and Sir Thomas Malory identified Tintagel as the birthplace of Arthur. Archaeologists from the University of Glasgow found remains of aristocratic dwellings of c. AD 500 – and a stone inscribed with the word 'Artognou'.

WINCHESTER

On the wall of Winchester's Great Hall is the top of a Round Table. Dating from about 1300, it may have been made on the orders of Edward I and was painted in heraldic style in 1522 on the orders of Henry VIII.

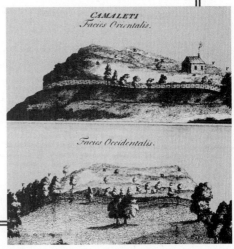

CAMALETI
Facies Orientalis.

Facies Occidentalis.

William of Malmesbury, a decade *before* Geoffrey, had noted that 'this Arthur is the hero of many wild tales...but assuredly deserves to be the object of reliable history rather than of false and dreaming fable'. However, this did nothing to stop Geoffrey's imaginative *History of the Kings of Britain* being a huge hit, widely plagiarized across Europe.

FURNISHING A SOLUTION

Frenchman Chrétien de Troyes, writing in *c.* 1170, added in courtly love, Camelot as a glittering capital, the quest for the Holy Grail and the Round Table. The table appears again around 1200 when Layamon produced the first Arthur tale in English, filling up 16,000 alliterative lines. According to Layamon, Arthur's Christmas revels were spoiled by quarrels over who should sit where at his table so he...

> *went to Cornwall and caused a marvellous table to be made by a carpenter, which had three remarkable properties; it could seat sixteen hundred; it was arranged that the high should be even with the low; it could be carried with Arthur wherever he wished to ride. The result was that all were satisfied.*

BONES AND BUILDING

In 1191 – that is, shortly after a disastrous fire in 1184 that had led to a massively expensive rebuilding programme – the alleged bones of Arthur were 'discovered' at Glastonbury Abbey. This was the same Glastonbury Abbey that claimed to have been founded by Joseph of Arimathea, the guardian of the Holy Grail.

In This Sign Conquer? A lead cross from Glastonbury, claimed to have belonged to King Arthur, the archetype of the Christian warrior against the forces of darkness.

THE ORDER OF THE GARTER

Legends such as that of King Arthur were critical in establishing the chivalric orders. The foremost order of this kind in England is The Most Noble Order of the Garter.

Membership is limited to 25 'Knights Companions' (including the Prince of Wales), plus the Sovereign as patron.

Foreigners may be admitted as 'extra knights'.

Thirty-six Garter Knights have been beheaded.

The Order's colours – gold on blue – allude to the royal arms of France.

The motto of the Order – *Honi soit qui mal y pense* (Shame on him who thinks ill of it) – refers to the royal slogan for Edward III's Crécy campaign of 1346.

Sir Winston Churchill refused the Garter after his electoral defeat in 1945 – 'I can hardly accept the Order of the Garter from the king after the people have given me the Order of the Boot.' He relented in 1953, as Prime Minister to the newly crowned Queen Elizabeth II.

ROYAL RESPECT

Edward I visited Glastonbury in 1278 to honour Arthur's supposed grave – just as he was conquering Wales outright. Perhaps this was an attempt to add an Arthurian lustre to his war – or maybe a heavy-handed gesture to remind the Welsh that their legendary hero was really dead.

In 1348 Edward III, described by a contemporary as 'unmatched since the days of Arthur, one-time King of England', was inspired to found the Order of the Garter (see above).

> *...the King...took pleasure to new rebuild the castle of Windsor, the which was begun by King Arthur; and there first began the Table Round, whereby sprang the fame of so many noble knights throughout all the world.*
>
> JEAN FROISSART, *CHRONICLES*

Later on, Henry VII, a Welshman with a shaky claim to England's throne, named his eldest son Arthur to bolster his new regime with a hijacked heritage.

THE LAST WORD?

Many readers today probably know the Arthur stories from Sir Thomas Malory's version, *Le Morte d'Arthur*. This was possibly compiled in around 1469 and was printed by William Caxton in 1485 – a timely prompt for Henry VII's exercise in royal rebranding.

Malory may have been one of several individuals but was probably a Warwickshire knight, charged with assault, theft and rape, who compiled his version of Arthur to kill time awaiting trial in a Southwark gaol. Confusingly Malory says the magic sword Excalibur was drawn from a stone *and* given to the king by the Lady of the Lake. Malory also predicted Arthur would one day return to rule Britain again:

> *Many men say that there is written on his tomb this verse:*
> *"Here lies Arthur: the once and future king".*

DEATH OF A HERO?

Arthur's legend peaked in the Middle Ages, and by the seventeenth century this figure who had once been revered throughout Christendom was only a hero in Britain. By the following century he was of interest only to antiquarians, but the nineteenth century saw a new revival of interest when William Dyce painted Arthurian scenes in the rebuilt Houses of Parliament. A little later, Alfred Tennyson's epic retelling of the Arthur legend, *The Idylls of the King*, gained cult status among Victorian readers.

Arthur was reborn yet again through T. H. White, former schoolmaster, recluse and expert on falconry. Beginning in 1939 with a children's book *The Sword in the Stone*, he followed up with a trilogy of adult novels, collectively published in 1958 as *The Once and Future*

King. This inspired the smash hit musical, *Camelot*. The most recent movie treatment has re-cast Arthur as a Roman cavalryman fighting to save Britain from brutal Saxons – which is where we came in.

✻ THE SAXON SETTLERS ✻

Behind the feet of the Legions and before the Northmen's ire,
Rudely but greatly begat they the body of state and shire.
RUDYARD KIPLING, *THE KING'S TASK*, 1911

The 'Anglo-Saxons' were initially different peoples – Angles, Saxons, Jutes and a few Frisians – from where modern-day Germany, Denmark and the Netherlands meet. What did they think they were coming to?

MOVING INTO A VACUUM?

There were Saxons living in 'Britannia' well before the Roman legions left, probably hired as mercenaries to fend off other Saxon pirates. Perhaps they told their relatives about Britain. The only contemporary authority for the arrival of the Anglo-Saxons in the fifth century is gloomy Gildas. According to him the Anglo-Saxons arrived in three ships – hardly an invasion fleet, especially as they brought their families with them. Nevertheless, he paints a picture of terrible devastation as a result of their arrival:

> *All the major towns were laid low... laid low, too, all the people... in the middle of the squares the foundation stones of high walls and towers... holy altars, fragments of corpses, covered with a purple crust of congealed blood, looked as though they had been churned up in some hellish wine-press. There was no burial to be had.*

Archaeology fails to support the Gildas apocalypse scenario, however. There are no remains of large-scale lethal confrontations between Romano-British forces and Anglo-Saxon intruders, nor anything to suggest a mass exodus of the existing population from the east to the west, seeking refuge from invading hordes.

If there was a drastic fall in Britain's population in the immediate post-Roman period – for example, caused by a major plague epidemic – newcomers might have been tempted by the prospect of an empty land.

SOME OF MY BEST FRIENDS ARE JUTES

In numbers, the Jutes were very much junior partners compared to the Angles and Saxons, but they kept a distinct identity, settling mainly in Kent, the Isle of Wight, and Hampshire around the Solent. This led to some curious anomalies:

- The Isle of Wight was the last part of England to accept Christianity – in 686, almost a century after Augustine had begun the conversion of Kent. ('Accept' probably isn't the right word – they were massacred until the survivors submitted.)

- The Jutish custom of partible inheritance (that is, property being divided equally among heirs rather than all going to the eldest) is said to account for Kent becoming a county of independent yeoman farmers rather than large estates.

- Tribal differences between the Jutes may also account for the establishment of separate dioceses for Canterbury and Rochester and the surviving distinction between 'Men of Kent' (born east of the Medway) and 'Kentish Men' (born to the west).

Opposite *The Mask of Monarchy: helmet of Raedwald, King of East Anglia, buried at Sutton Hoo, Suffolk, c. 624-25. Decorated with gold fittings and garnets from India, it was the work of a Scandinavian master.*

COEXISTENCE AND CONVERSION

The newcomers arrived as pagans, who cremated or buried their dead with grave goods for the afterlife. Christians did not do either, but instead interred corpses in an east–west orientation. Large concentrations of pagan burials and an absence of Christian ones would imply the displacement of one population by another. Instead we find pagan and Christian burials of the same date at the same locations, implying an overlap of belief systems or at least a coexistence.

Anglo-Saxons brought distinctive forms of dress and adornment, pottery and weaponry, building styles and ceremonial observances. Gradually these 'English' ways and the 'English' language became dominant everywhere except what was now 'the Celtic fringe'. However, this did not necessarily happen by force: the new ways were also adopted voluntarily by people eager for a lifestyle better adapted to an abandoned imperial outpost. This was cultural conquest, not so much by invasion as by imitation.

WAR WORDS

On the other hand Anglo-Saxon vocabulary *was* distinctly bloodthirsty (even the word itself is a compound of two Anglo-Saxon words). The tenth-century epic poem *The Battle of Maldon* runs to only 325 lines but includes more than 70 different words to do with fighting – plus almost 40 for prince or leader. There are seventeen synonyms for warrior (spear-bearer, retainer, slaughterous wolf), a dozen for battle, ten for army or troop, eight for spear and four for sword. Only about ten of the terms survive in modern language – the rest were largely replaced by words from the victorious Normans.

THE VILLAGE PEOPLE

Another possible scenario is that the Anglo-Saxons came in small numbers but operated an apartheid system and outbred whoever their laws defined as inferior. These unfortunates were called the *wealhas*, a word equating foreigner and slave (and which has survived in the word 'Welsh').

The Anglo-Saxons were farmers, not city-slickers. Although they did found trading-ports at Hamwic (Southampton), Norwich, Ipswich and Sandwich, they were largely responsible for the thousands of villages whose names include the elements *-ing* (people of), *-ham* (home) or *-ton* (settlement) – many of which are now embedded in vast cities like London, as in Balham, Peckham, Ealing, Barking, Islington or Kensington.

LAYING DOWN THE LAW

Victorian scholars celebrated the Anglo-Saxon origins of the Common Law to stress its antiquity and continuity. To modern eyes its ancient practices may seem less appealing:

- Apart from political prisoners, imprisonment was rare. Routine punishments included fines, mutilation and banishment.

- Equality before the law was an alien notion. There were different rights for different social categories, such as assimilated Welshmen.

- To prevent blood-feuds, injuries were compensated by the payment of *wergild*, which varied with social rank. The loss of an eye or hand by a landowning thegn was reckoned to be worth six times as much as a similar injury done to a mere ceorl or freeman.

THE MONK WHO INVENTED
✤ THE ENGLISH ✤

Historia Ecclesia Gentis Anglorum (*The Ecclesiastical History of the English Peoples*) is hardly a snappy title but it was a historical milestone, because it spoke of the English as a single people. It also made its author, Bede, the greatest historian for five centuries either side of his lifetime. The sparse details Bede tacked on about his own life also make him the first Englishman to write an autobiography.

Bede spent his whole life in the twin monasteries of Jarrow and Monkwearmouth, never venturing further than York, but was famed for his learning across Christendom. Although he did not invent it, it was Bede who popularized the notion of AD – 'Anno Domini' – the idea that Christ's birth divided all history. ('BC' – 'Before Christ' – said in English, not Latin, was a back formation, only coined in the eighteenth century.)

GOING SOMEWHERE

Bede's *Ecclesiastical History* was completed in around 731, near the end of his life. It was less an account of events than of their significance, addressed to a people and posterity.

Documenting the conversion to Christianity of the English, the *History* was intended to provide both a record of the past and an inspiration for the future. This was a history with a *direction* – driven by the idea that the Angles, Saxons and Jutes constituted one people, the English, and that they could be united into one Christian kingdom under one ruler.

Bede's *History* also aims to show that events prove God's power. It aims at accuracy, not objectivity. Don't expect a fair-minded account of paganism. Written for a warrior people, it proclaims a good Christian life as the best guarantee of victory. A most memorable passage described faith as the answer to man's ignorance of his own life's purpose:

> *The present life of men on earth, O king, compared with time*
> *unknowable, seems like this…as if, sitting at dinner with your chiefs in*
> *wintertime…a sparrow from outside flew swiftly through the hall…in*
> *that time it is untouched by the storm; but…in a moment…it soon*
> *returns to the winter and slips from sight. Man's life appears like*
> *that…of what may follow it, or what preceded it, we know nothing.*

NORTHERN LIGHTS

Bede was the flower of a 'Northumbrian Renaissance', which also produced the exquisite Lindisfarne Gospels (see opposite). He owed his own education to the library amassed by Benedict Biscop, the aristocratic founder of Bede's monastery, who had rejected Celtic frugality in favour of Mediterranean magnificence, importing stonemasons and glaziers from Gaul. At the other end of the social scale was Caedmon, a cowherd with the miraculous ability to turn Bible stories into simple Saxon songs.

Alongside his *History*, Bede wrote the biography of the hermit St Cuthbert, whose grave was credited with many miracles (see opposite). Bede is also the chief source for the life of St Egbert,

Desk jockey: through his prolific writings monastery-bound Bede established a scholarly reputation throughout Europe and down the centuries.

IN THE BEGINNING WAS THE WORD...

The Lindisfarne Gospels constitute the first Christian scripture in English – though that was not why they were originally made. Lindisfarne, also known as Holy Island, lies a mile off the Northumberland coast, making it attractively isolated for a monastery. One of its most distinguished residents was the reclusive, austere St Cuthbert, successively prior, hermit and bishop, who died there in 687.

Cuthbert's grave drew pilgrims even before his corpse was translated to a grand tomb in 698. The making of the Lindisfarne Gospels was probably linked with that event. The calligrapher was probably Eadfrith, Cuthbert's successor as bishop.

Reading between the lines: initial page from the opening chapter of the Gospel according to St Mark.

THE BOOK

Each Gospel – Matthew, Mark, Luke and John – is preceded by a page portrait of the saintly author, a 'carpet' page incorporating Anglo-Saxon, Insular ('Celtic') and Byzantine motifs, and a page for the initial letter of the following text. The work took about three years to complete, not including the labour in making hundreds of vellum pages from sheepskins, preparing inks and paints and creating the elaborate, jewelled binding.

THE JOURNEY

Foreshadowed by violent storms, in 875 Viking raids led the monks to abandon Lindisfarne. Wandering the mainland with Cuthbert's corpse and their treasured Gospels, the monks eventually settled in Chester-le-Street. Here, in around 960, an Anglo-Saxon translation in Northumbrian dialect and penned in reddish ink was inserted between the lines of the Latin text by Aldred of Chester-le-Street.

THE OUTCOME

Cuthbert was finally laid to rest in Durham Cathedral in 995. As with many of England's early saints, his shrine was vandalized at the Dissolution and the cover of the Gospels torn off for its embellishments.

another Northumbrian, who established the cathedral school of York. One of Egbert's own pupils, St Willibrord, converted the fierce Frisians and became Archbishop of Utrecht. Willibrord's protégé, St Boniface, led the conversion to Christianity of Germany. Alcuin, another Northumbrian and product of the York school became a one-man think-tank to the great Charlemagne, in his court at Aachen.

LEGACY

Viking raids forced the abandonment of Jarrow and Monkwearmouth in about 800. Bede's alleged remains were discovered in the eleventh century and moved to Durham Cathedral, where they now lie in the subdued splendour of the Galilee Chapel. By the ninth century Bede was already referred to as 'Venerabilis', but it was only in 1899 that Pope Leo XIII formally recognized this venerable historian as a doctor of the church.

✳ THE ONE, THE ONLY... ✳

Alfred of Wessex is the only English king to be called 'the Great' but is best remembered for burning some cakes.

The Victorians, however, hailed him as the founder of the navy and the saviour of the nation. As far as they were concerned, without Alfred there wouldn't have been an England at all. Alfred also raised English to the dignity of a learned language and was the first monarch to write a book. The next was Henry VIII, some six centuries later.

To mark the thousandth anniversary of Alfred's death in 899 a statue was raised in his memory at Winchester, the capital of his kingdom. The king is portrayed as a beefy warrior raising a mighty sword in triumph – but holding it point downward, like a Christian cross. A wheezing figure hunched over a book by candlelight would have been nearer the reality. Throughout his life Alfred battled with constant illnesses, possibly including epilepsy.

WESSEX WARRIOR

In 871, the year he became king, a see-saw struggle with the Vikings took the kingdom of Wessex to the brink of extinction. Alfred fled to the Somerset marshes around Athelney and somehow managed to raise an army and win a hard-fought victory at Ethandune (Edington) in 878 – a date to stand beside 1588, 1805 and 1940 as an hour of deliverance.

Alfred then astounded his enemies by *not* massacring them. Instead he stood godfather to their leader, Guthrum, who accepted Christianity and the division of England along an agreed frontier. Alfred then stabilized what he had saved by creating some 30 fortified *burhs*, each within a day's march of another for mutual support.

To garrison the *burhs* Alfred reorganized the *fyrd* (militia) to serve in rotation so that the harvest was not neglected. Manpower needs were precisely calculated to allow for four spearmen to defend each pole (= 16.6 feet) of defensive circuit – plus another tenth as a mobile reserve. As we learn from the *Anglo-Saxon Chronicle*, a fleet of super-sized ships was built to take the fight to the Vikings by sea: 'Some had 60 oars, some more. They were both swifter…and also higher than the others…'.

BURHS INTO BOROUGHS

Once their strategic purpose was over, these *burhs* suffered various fates. Some, like Bath, Chichester and Winchester, were revivals of Roman sites and resumed city status. Some, like Oxford and Stamford, grew into significant settlements, or modest market towns like Shaftesbury and Malmesbury. Others, like Lydford, Halwell and Pilton in Devon and Lyng, Langport and Axbridge in Somerset, declined into villages. At Wallingford and Wareham both the original street-plan and features of the Saxon defences are still visible.

In 886 the abandoned walled city of Roman Londinium was repopulated and refortified to become Lundenburgh, marking the beginning of London's continuous existence ever since.

OUR STORY... BY OURSELVES

The *Anglo-Saxon Chronicle* is the first history of a European people written by themselves in their own language, rather than in Latin. Begun on the orders of King Alfred, the surviving versions of the *Anglo-Saxon Chronicle* together constitute the single most important source for the early history of England.

CONTENTS LIST

Drawing on the work of Bede, other annals, genealogies and lists of kings and bishops, the authors compiled a chronology down to their own times and then recorded what they regarded as significant contemporary events.

The peaceable years of the mid-tenth century receive much less attention than the long and troubled reign of Aethelred the Unready. The *Chronicle* is also excellent for the reign of Edward the Confessor (1042–66) and some versions go up to the mid-twelfth century.

SIX SURVIVALS

Of the seven known manuscripts, one was almost completely destroyed in a fire in 1731 – but fortunately had already been transcribed. The other six are known by letters:

The oldest, Ms. A, was written, probably at Winchester, by a single hand up to the year 891, then in various hands until 975, then tampered with at Canterbury. It is now at Corpus Christi College, Cambridge.

Mss. B and C, in the British Library, are copies made at Abingdon.

Ms. F, also in the British Library, is an abridgement in English and Latin.

Mss. D and E, now at the Bodleian Library in Oxford, incorporate much material about the north of England.

Ms. E, made at Peterborough, was written as a single stretch up to 1121 and then kept up until 1155, giving a famous account of the anarchy of the reign of King Stephen, 'when men said openly that Christ and his saints slept...'.

The *Chronicle* incorporates a triumphant eulogy for the greatest battle of the Anglo-Saxon age. Fought in 937 at Brunanburh – an unknown, probably Northumbrian, location – it saw Athelstan annihilate an allied force of Vikings and Scots:

> Never yet in this island
> was there a greater slaughter
> of peoples felled by the sword's
> edges.

Opposite *The Alfred Jewel, recovered by miraculous chance in 1693.*

PROMOTING THE LANGUAGE

Law codes, incorporating elements from Kent and Mercia, were consolidated into a single corpus.

Alfred himself, by the age of 40, had mastered both Latin and English. To repair the Viking devastation of monasteries, the chief centres of learning, Alfred inaugurated a programme of translations from Latin into English of books 'most necessary for all men to know'.

> …all the youth now in England of free men, who are rich enough to be
> able to devote themselves to it, be set to learn as long as they are not fit
> for any other occupation, until they are able to read English writing well.
>
> ALFRED THE GREAT, PREFACE TO *PASTORAL CURE*

Gregory the Great's *Pastoral Care* was promoted as a manual for bishops. Each copy was accompanied by a magnificent gold enamelled aestel (pointer). The handle of one, now known as the 'Alfred Jewel', was miraculously found in a Somerset marsh and is on display in Oxford's Ashmolean Museum. Bede's *Ecclesiastical History* provided a historical justification for the king's own efforts as a defender of church and state.

A LEGEND IN HIS LIFETIME

By the 890s Alfred, King of Wessex, was calling himself 'King of the Angles and Saxons'. Coins show him wearing a diadem like a Roman emperor. Charters refer to him as 'King of the English'. Neighbouring, formerly rival, Mercia acknowledged his overlordship, as did all the English not under Danish rule.

When the Vikings returned to the attack in 892 they were beaten back, with most of four years of fighting taking place outside the territory of the West Saxons.

The kingdom held.

WHO WAS THE FIRST KING OF ENGLAND?

Though Alfred of Wessex was referred to as 'King of the English', in reality he was only king of the English not under Danish control.

AFTER ALFRED

Alfred's son, Edward the Elder (reigned 899–924), captured the five Danish-held boroughs of Leicester, Stamford, Nottingham, Derby and Lincoln, and annexed Mercia – thus controlling all England south of the Humber. Edward's eldest son, Athelstan (reigned 924–39), took Danish-held York and received the homage of the rulers of Wales and Scotland. Athelstan also issued a fine coinage for national circulation, styling himself *Rex totius Britanniae* – King of all Britain.

> *We declare... that there shall be one coinage throughout the king's dominions and that there shall be no minting except in a port. And if a minter be convicted of striking bad money, the hand with which he was guilty shall be cut off and set up on his smithy.*
>
> LAWS OF ATHELSTAN

Athelstan's half-brother, Edmund, also known as the Elder (reigned 939–46), succeeded him at eighteen and was dead at 25. Although he conducted successful campaigns against the Vikings in the Midlands and Northumbria, he lost control of York.

Pious Edred (reigned 946–55), brother of Edmund, reclaimed York and took Northumbria when its Danish ruler, the picturesquely named Eric Bloodaxe, was killed in battle in 954. Edred carelessly died unmarried, aged 32, so he was followed by his 15-year-old nephew, Edwy the Fair (reigned 955–59), son of Edmund. Edwy proved weak and incompetent, capable only of holding on to Wessex, while Mercia and Northumbria were ruled by his successor, Edgar. Edwy's death at 19 (he was probably murdered) was less a disaster than a release.

EDGAR, CROWNED KING

The name of Edgar (reigned 959–75) means 'rich in spears' but he became known as 'the Peaceable'. The grandson of Alfred, teenage Edgar inherited a stable realm, free from threat.

Edgar enthusiastically supported St Dunstan, Archbishop of Canterbury, in re-establishing monasteries as centres of learning. Edgar also won over his subjects in the formerly Danish east and north of England.

However, Edgar's coronation was deferred for fourteen years. Why precisely this should be, we don't know. Perhaps the king's extramarital track record may have required years of penance and patronage to work off. Perhaps Dunstan wanted Edgar to prove himself and his commitment to reviving the Church.

Whatever the reason, by the time of his coronation Edgar had passed 30, then the lowest customary age for becoming a priest (since Christ's ministry began when he was 30).

Edgar's predecessors were formally recognized at Kingston-on-Thames, in a procedure that was more an administrative than a ceremonial occasion. Edgar was installed as monarch at Bath Abbey, the first to be *crowned* 'King of the English'; his wife, Elfrida, was crowned 'Queen of the English'. Orchestrated by Dunstan on 11 May 873 (Whit Sunday), Edgar's coronation was modelled on the installation of a Holy Roman Emperor and established the basic pattern for all coronations ever since.

To emphasize the sacral nature of kingship, the solemn pledges Edgar gave to protect the Church and uphold the law were followed by an anointing to symbolize his priestly status. To emphasize the unity of the kingdom Dunstan shared the ceremony with Oswald, Archbishop of York, by birth a Dane.

Edgar's coronation was noted by all contemporary chroniclers, inspired a national ballad and is commemorated in Bath Abbey today by a stained-glass window.

UNHAPPY SUCCESSORS

In terms of royal authority, however, Edgar's magnificent coronation marked a false dawn, since the king died just two years later. Edgar's eldest son and successor, a mere lad of 12 or 13, was crowned by Dunstan at Kingston-on-Thames but lured to his assassination by his stepmother and is remembered as 'Edward the Martyr'.

Her son, Edward's half-brother, a boy of just ten or 11, would rule for nearly 40 years – disastrously – as Aethelred II (reigned 978–1016), 'the Unready' – a reference, not to habitual tardiness but to his lack of 'raed', wise counsel or advice. Despite serial disasters and humiliations, however, England henceforth held together as one kingdom.

BY GEORGE!

> *George was... a rich noble under the cruel emperor... Datian, in the province of Cappadocia.... Datian... commanded that George be hung on a gibbet and his limbs torn with iron claws, and torches kindled on both sides... after that... to be tortured with scourges and rubbed with salt; but George remained unhurt.... Thereupon Datian endited this decree, "Take this guilty one... and drag him prone... through all the... stony ways".*
>
> AELFRIC, *LIVES OF THE SAINTS*

After which, apparently, it was still necessary to cut his head off with a sword. 'Datian' – the Roman emperor Diocletian – was then struck dead by lightning going home. This version of the martyrdom of St George was written by the English monk Aelfric in about 1000 – with absolutely no mention of a dragon.

WHO'S WHO?

Edward Gibbon, author of *The Decline and Fall of the Roman Empire*, uncharitably identified St George as a blackmarketeering archbishop of Cappadocia who was strangled by a mob.

LIFE OF A LEGEND

George's adoption as patron saint of England occurred only gradually:

700s St George mentioned by Bede.

800s A church dedicated to George is referred to in the will of Alfred the Great.

1098 Crusaders besieging Antioch swear that St George gave them a hand.

1190 The City of London adopts his flag for its ships in the Mediterranean to show they were under Genoese protection.

1222 The Synod of Oxford decrees that his day, 23 April, should be observed as a feast.

1265–66 The saint's story is consolidated in the *Golden Legend* composed by Jacobus de Voragine, Archbishop of Genoa. This tells how George rescued the daughter of a Libyan king from a dragon and in gratitude the king's subjects became Christians.

1348 Edward III adopts the saint as patron of his new Order of the Garter – and he has remained England's hero ever since.

A modern consensus suggests that St George was a high-ranking aristocratic soldier of Diocletian's personal guard who was martyred for refusing to renounce Christianity. He was probably born in around 275 in Nicomedia (modern-day Izmit in Turkey) and died in 303 at Lydda (Lod, in Israel).

The one certain thing about England's patron saint is that he wasn't English. Which may partly explain why he is, or has also been, the patron of Portugal, Genoa, Georgia, Greece, Aragon, Catalonia, Ethiopia, Lithuania, Palestine, Russia, at least fourteen cities, archers, armourers and shepherds, sufferers from herpes, leprosy and syphilis, the Norwegian cavalry, Corinthian FC of São Paulo and the Boy Scouts of America.

2
LOST LANDSCAPES

*…once, on this familiar ground, walked other men and
women, as actual as we are today…but now all gone,
one generation vanishing after another, gone as
utterly as we ourselves shall shortly be gone.*
G. M. TREVELYAN, *CLIO, A MUSE*, 1913

*Trackway and Camp and City lost,
Salt Marsh where now is corn –
Old Wars, Old Peace, Old Arts that cease,
And so was England born!*
RUDYARD KIPLING, *PUCK OF POOK'S HILL*, 1906

A famous series of Second World War recruiting posters, aimed at the most urbanized population in the world, featured views of the English countryside (Sussex, in fact) to represent what was at stake in the struggle for national survival.

The image of an unchanging English environment is, of course, a misrepresentation of a much more complicated story of transformations shaped by centuries of effort, enterprise, greed and folly.

THE LARGEST ARCHAEOLOGICAL
✵ MONUMENT IN ENGLAND ✵

Twice as long as Hadrian's Wall but not half so well known, Offa's Dyke is the largest and, in engineering terms, most demanding earthwork in European history. Running from the Dee to the Severn, right along the border with Wales, it was built on the orders of Offa, King of Mercia (reigned 757–96).

MERCIAN DOMINANCE

Offa made Mercia the most powerful English kingdom, conquering Kent, Sussex, Essex and East Anglia, annexing parts of Powys and styling himself 'Rex Anglorum' – King of the English. He also persuaded the Church to found a new archbishopric in the Mercian heartland, at Lichfield.

Offa's coins are the most numerous issued by any Anglo-Saxon king and established the penny as the basic unit of exchange in England. Offa's image on the penny is based on the biblical King David. The gold coinage has OFFA REX (Offa the King) inside an Arabic inscription copied from a dinar issued by the Abbasid Caliph Al-Mansur in 774.

To assure the succession of his chosen heir, Ecgfrith, in 787 Offa installed him as his co-ruler. This proved futile. Following Offa's death Ecgfrith reigned for just 141 days. Chroniclers interpreted this as a divine judgment on Offa's own bloodstained career. Mercia rapidly lost its pre-eminence and the archbishopric of Lichfield was abolished.

Profile of power: a silver penny issued by Offa the Great. His son Ecgfrith was the first whose coronation involved anointing with holy oil – to no protective effect, apparently.

OFFA'S MONUMENT

Offa's Dyke, however, has survived – or at least some 80 miles of it. Built just to the west of an older fortification, Wat's Dyke, it consists of a 6-foot-deep ditch fronting a rampart originally 25 feet high and up to 60 feet across. Parts may have been surmounted by a wooden palisade or even a stone wall.

The work would have required tens of thousands of labourers, a formidable organizational effort for a regime still largely illiterate. Although the work's alignment with the landscape makes maximum use of its defensive potential, the actual construction shows none of the quality and consistency achieved by the Roman builders of Hadrian's Wall. Probably the work was delegated to local leaders and their reluctant followers.

FRONTIER OR FORTIFICATION?

Sir Cyril Fox, who made extensive excavations of the site in the 1930s, believed Offa's Dyke represented an agreed frontier with the Welsh.

However, more recent work by the University of Manchester contradicts this, affirming Offa's Dyke as a barrier against Welsh attempts to recover lost lands. The fact that the earthwork always protrudes west of any hills, providing a clear view into Welsh territory, suggests it was there to hinder raiders from driving off livestock and deter full-scale invasions.

Whatever Offa's Dyke once meant it is now a popular walking route. Opened in 1971, the Offa's Dyke Path runs some 180 miles from Prestatyn via Llangollen, Montgomery and Hay-on-Wye to Chepstow, and is followed each year by some 9,000 walkers.

CITY BENEATH THE SEA

The history of the city of Dunwich is a chronicle of refusal to surrender – or possibly to face facts.

632 St Felix of Burgundy establishes Dunwich, the chief seaport of the east coast of England, as the seat of the first bishopric of East Anglia.

1086 The Domesday survey records Dunwich as having 3,000 inhabitants and six churches and being worth £50 a year to the king – plus 60,000 herrings.

1199 Chartered as a borough, Dunwich becomes an important religious centre with two monasteries, a hospital and 18 churches and chapels.

1286 City suffers a major sea surge.

1295 Dunwich sends two representatives to the 'Model Parliament' convened by Edward I. But this thriving community of 5,000 inhabitants was already under attack from the sea.

1328 A storm overwhelms 400 houses and three churches, leaving the harbour cut off, to the great benefit of rival Walberswick.

1347 Another major storm is followed by the Black Death.

1570 Further flooding as the coastal erosion continues inexorably.

1677 This time the flood reaches the marketplace.

1700s Dunwich sends two Members to Parliament, even though it has only eight residents qualified to vote.

1832 The Reform Act abolishes 'rotten boroughs'.

1886 The corporation of the 'town' is abolished.

1904 The body of the last medieval church, All Saints, is reclaimed by the sea, its tower finally falling in 1919.

Seals of the burgesses of Dunwich.

Today, fragments remain only of Greyfriars' monastery and its associated leper hospital, which was founded sometime before 1277 and then moved inland some time after 1290. Today, if you want to visit Dunwich you'll need a snorkel.

✳ LANDSCAPE OF CONQUEST ✳

England's on the anvil – hear the hammers ring –
Clanging from the Severn to the Tyne!
Never was the blacksmith like our Norman king –
England's being hammered, hammered into line.

RUDYARD KIPLING, *THE ANVIL*, 1911

The Romans imported their idea of a state. In 1066 the Normans simply took over an existing one. The arrogance of their rule was made brutally clear by its impact on the landscape. Castles, cathedrals and the royal forest reserve symbolized the imposition of an alien power.

THE NORMANS' SECRET WEAPON

William the Conqueror's expeditionary force of 7,000, reinforced by a trickle of migrants, managed to hold down a conquered population of two million or more.

A key factor in their success was the construction of castles.

He caused castles to be built
Which were a sore burden to the poor,
A hard man was the king....

ANGLO-SAXON CHRONICLE

The Anglo-Saxons knew about fortifications but built them for whole communities, as in the case of Alfred's *burhs*. Norman castles were far smaller – and far more numerous.

The Bayeux Tapestry shows a prefabricated fort the Normans brought with them. In fact they brought three. These provided the model for the first generation of castles, which consisted of a mound (motte) of earth, surmounted by a palisade of wood, and fronted by a fenced courtyard (bailey) for essential outbuildings like stables.

The motte-and-bailey castle, constructed from local materials by forced labour, could be thrown up in weeks and was vulnerable only

Section of the Bayeux Tapestry showing (centre) Normans throwing up an earth motte to support a prefabricated castle. To the right the invaders announce their arrival by firing local housing to goad the Saxons into fighting.

to trained and determined attackers. By the time the Domesday survey was made in 1086 the Normans had built 86 stone castles – and a thousand wooden ones.

GOD'S FORTRESSES

You might see churches rise in every village, and, in the towns and cities, monasteries built after a style unknown before; you could watch the country flourishing with renewed religious observance...
WILLIAM OF MALMESBURY

William I got the Pope's blessing to conquer England by promising to reform its Church – which in real terms meant putting it more firmly under Rome's control and purging it of local customs.

After the conquest, William duly filled the top church positions with foreigners, and started a crash building programme so that by 1100 every cathedral had been, or was being, rebuilt.

The Normans usually demolished an existing Anglo-Saxon cathedral and replaced it with another, usually larger, one on or near the same site. In half a dozen cases, however, they abandoned the location altogether, as at North Elmham in Norfolk and Sherborne in Dorset.

St Wulfstan of Worcester, the last surviving Anglo-Saxon bishop, did not share William of Malmesbury's priorities: 'We poor wretches destroy the works of our forefathers only to get praise to ourselves. The happy age of holy men knew not how to build stately churches…but we neglect the care of souls and labour to heap up stones.'

'WASTA EST'

No impact on the English landscape was more dramatic than the 'Harrying of the North' by vengeful Normans after an attempted uprising in 1069. Most of what peasants needed to see them through the winter – stocks of grain, livestock, wooden hovels and farm tools – was utterly destroyed by fire and sword. A swathe of territory, centred on Yorkshire, was devastated so completely that perhaps 100,000 people were slaughtered or starved. Twenty years later the Domesday survey would write of scores of formerly thriving villages: 'wasta est' – it is waste.

FORESTS

Anglo-Saxon kings had often had favoured areas for hunting but William the Conqueror created a strict and savage regime of formal regulation. Henceforth 'forest' would mean any area designated as subject to 'Forest Law', whether woodland, heath, cultivated fields or even whole towns, like Waltham Abbey, which lay within the 60,000 acres of Waltham Forest.

This Forest Law was designed to protect both game and its environment, and was enforced by a hierarchy of special courts, served by a specialized police of wardens and 'verderers'. The *Anglo-Saxon Chronicle* makes it clear how seriously this was taken:

> He set apart a vast deer preserve and imposed laws concerning it.
> Whoever slew a hart or a hind
> Was to be blinded…
> For he loved the stags as dearly
> As though he had been their father.

The creation of these forests was often no less brutal. William of Malmesbury, the son of a Norman father and English (Anglo-Saxon) mother, described how the Conqueror had created a 'New Forest' in Hampshire, destroying whole villages 'for more than thirty miles around – a dreadful sight…once where there had been human activity and the worship of God, deer now ranged unrestrained, animals of no real value to mankind.'

Deer were, in fact, highly prized as meat for the royal table. A letter from Henry III, dated 4 September 1251, contains an order for William Luvel and Henry de Candour, the 'king's huntsmen', to take '60 bucks in the king's Forest of Dean', as well as another 60 from the New Forest 'to be salted and transported to London for the forthcoming feast of St Edmund.'

However, the forest could provide many other sources of income and materials, including wood (for building timber, fences and hurdles or as bark or charcoal), grazing land for cattle, pigs and sheep, mineral deposits (for example, coal and iron in the Forest of Dean), payments for 'assarting' (clearing a patch of land for cultivation), and fines for infringements of Forest Law. While offenders could be mutilated, most monarchs preferred money, though dogs were crippled to prevent their use in poaching.

… AND MORE FORESTS

At the time of the Domesday survey in 1086 there were two dozen forests. A century later, during the reign of Henry II, almost a third of England was designated as 'forest'. The distribution was highly uneven, however: for example, all of Essex was forest but none of Hertfordshire, Kent, Sussex or Cornwall.

In 1204 the people of Devon paid King John the fabulous sum of 5,000 marks to disafforest their county – apart from Dartmoor and Exmoor. Royal forests were particularly numerous in Somerset, Derbyshire and north-east Yorkshire. By the time the aristocratic discontent expressed in Magna Carta (1215) brought a virtual end to the creation of new forests, almost 150 had been created. There were still 69 royal forests around 1330 but by then the crown had gained a more secure source of income from taxing wool exports and Forest Law became less rigorously enforced.

There were also other classes of forests. 'Chases', for example, were private, rather than royal, forests; there were at least thirty of these. 'Parks', of which there were over 3,000, were hunting areas stocked with deer. Usually of 100 to 200 acres, these were enclosed by a 'pale' (a protective ditch and bank topped with a wall, fence or hedge) to keep game in and poachers and predators out.

Former royal forests often retained a reputation as something of a world apart. Tudor historian William Camden wrote of the Forest of Dean as:

> *a wonderful thick forest and in former ages so dark and*
> *terrible, by reason of crooked and winding ways,*
> *as also the grisly shade therein, that it made the*
> *inhabitants more fierce and bolder to commit robberies.*

ENDURING RIGHTS

Both the Forest of Dean and the New Forest still have a Court of Verderers. The Forest of Dean's Court meets every 40 days at Coleford in the 'Speech House', which is now also a hotel. Inhabitants of the New Forest still have rights of:

- Estover (cutting firewood)
- Marl (improving the soil)
- Pannage (letting pigs forage for acorns)
- Pasturage (grazing livestock)
- Turbary (cutting turf for fuel)

LONG-EARED LUXURY

The hare is native to Britain but the rabbit was introduced by the Normans, possibly from Spain, in around 1100. In fact, it took a couple of centuries for rabbits to adapt completely to local conditions, so the early importations had to be cosseted with winter feed and by having mounds of soft earth raised for them to burrow into.

Strictly speaking the term rabbit only referred to the young, the mature animal being known as a 'coney'. Valued for their meat as a delicacy and for their fur as a luxury garment lining, rabbits were raised in warrens with protected boundaries, guarded by warreners who lived in fortified lodges to protect them from bands of poachers.

These warrens were an important feature of the royal forests of Ashdown, Hatfield, Epping and Dartmoor. In the Breckland region, where there were a dozen major warrens, they were an important component of the local economy. Lakenheath Warren, belonging to the Prior of Ely, was ten miles round, covering more than 2,000 acres and producing 25,000 rabbits a year.

✸ THE LOST VILLAGES OF ENGLAND ✸

Fornham St Genevieve, Hungry Bentley and Wharram Percy – village names you might think were made up for tourists. But names are all they now have.

WHERE NOT TO LIVE

More than three thousand 'deserted villages' are scattered, *apparently* very unevenly, across the English countryside. Norfolk, Northamptonshire, Warwickshire and Shropshire each have more than 100. Buckinghamshire has more than 80, Hertfordshire more than 70.

CLASSIC CASE STUDY

The most thoroughly investigated of deserted villages, excavated annually from 1948 to 1990, is Wharram Percy, in the Yorkshire Wolds. The figures show how it spent centuries on the edge of extinction:

1086 'Warron' has 35 houses, including two manor houses, set out in neat rows with regular garden plots, plus two watermills and a fish pond.

1323 Only 18 households were inhabited.

1349 The Black Death cuts the population by a third to 45.

1368 After a second plague epidemic in 1361, some 30 houses are again occupied.

1458 Just 16 houses are occupied.

1500s Only four families remain in the village; they were then evicted by the landowner, Baron Hylton, in order to convert the village fields from arable cultivation to sheep-rearing.

Today Wharram Percy is in the care of English Heritage and may be visited.

There are even 26 on the Isle of Wight. But only 7 have been identified in Essex, just 4 in Surrey and none in Middlesex.

Some deserted villages, like Chysauster and Trewortha in Cornwall, date back to the Iron Age but most were established and abandoned in the Middle Ages.

The excavation of deserted sites opens a window into a distant past uncluttered by the leavings of later periods. The rarity of coin finds in medieval villages, for example, confirms how much they depended on barter and exchange, rather than cash.

Upton in Gloucestershire, first mentioned in a charter of the ninth century, has also been the object of long-term investigation. In 1299 there were 16 tenant households at Upton but by 1327 only four; by 1384 the village was completely deserted. So far 29 buildings, distributed over a 12-acre site, have been uncovered. The most disturbing find has been the discovery of a baby's skeleton beneath the floor of a house. This is very rare; the reason can only be guessed at.

DEATH SENTENCES

Plague was only one of several possible reasons for deserting a previously viable site. In the twelfth century monks of the new Cistercian order cleared away inconvenient settlements in the sparsely populated north of England to create vast sheep-runs to sustain their abbeys. The foundation of Revesby Abbey in Lincolnshire in 1143, for example, resulted in the extinction of three entire settlements.

Climatic deterioration in the early fourteenth century led to the abandonment of marginal settlements on heaths and moors. Hound Tor on Dartmoor was one such. Inhabited on and off since the Bronze Age, 'Hundatora' was reoccupied by the tenth century and in the thirteenth century had at least 11 buildings including three 'longhouses' for peasants and their livestock, and three barns for drying grain.

Marginal locations such as Hound Tor were also abandoned as an indirect consequence of the plague, since the destruction of entire communities – as at Tilgarsley and Tismore in Oxfordshire and Hall and Ellington in Northamptonshire – freed up fertile land, causing migration of survivors.

SUBSTITUTING SHEEP

The loss of labour to epidemics in the fourteenth century raised wages so much that landlords turned to farming wool rather than wheat, replacing ploughmen and oxen with (more economical) boys and dogs. By the sixteenth century, the sheep began to take over:

Your sheep which are usually so tame…are now…so greedy and wild that they devour men and lay waste…fields, houses and towns…nobles and gentlemen and even holy abbots…enclose every bit of land for pasture…leaving only the church to pen the sheep in.

SIR THOMAS MORE, *UTOPIA*, 1516

Ingarsby in Leicestershire was largely taken over by Leicester Abbey in 1354, after the Black Death. Systematic buying put the abbey in complete control by 1469 when Ingarsby was finally emptied of humans and given over to sheep. Another Leicestershire settlement, Holyoak, had its population reduced from 200 households to just 30 inhabitants, the rest evicted in 1496 to make way for sheep and cattle.

In 1489 Parliament passed the first of several Acts to prohibit the deliberate depopulation of established communities but the movement continued relentlessly as England switched from exporting raw wool to even bigger profits from exporting woollen cloth.

PARKS AND PROSPECTS

A parallel motive for wiping out entire settlements was the desire of a landowner to create a park, either for hunting in, or simply to have something nice to look onto.

Henry VIII did the former at Nonsuch (see pp. 55–58). The Earl of Carlisle, Charles Howard, did the latter to create Castle Howard in Yorkshire. This eliminated the village of Henderskelf so completely that no trace of either its church or its castle remained when Channel 4's popular archaeology programme *Time Team* attempted to rediscover them.

The Saxon settlement of Godwich in Norfolk was bought by the ruthless lawyer Sir Edward Coke in 1580. Within five years he had built an imposing brick manor house and monster barn right across what had been the village street. A map of 1596 labels numerous plots as 'formerly built upon', and in the seventeenth century the church was pulled down and its materials recycled to make a folly in the form of a church tower.

At Nuneham Courtney, near Oxford, the Harcourt family demolished an existing village that would have spoiled the prospect from their new residence, Nuneham House. In 1761 they rehoused their dispossessed tenants in a model village with a main street of identical

Arcadian idyll – but probably not for the gardeners. Artfully planted parks like the one at Nuneham Courtney required the constant labour of small armies of labourers to keep them looking 'natural'.

double cottages. They also replaced the medieval church with a Neo-classical temple designed by James 'Athenian' Stuart and had the grounds landscaped by Lancelot 'Capability' Brown. The rector used the gravestones from the old churchyard to pave the garden of his new rectory. This drastic demonstration of landlord *machismo* inspired Oliver Goldsmith's poem of protest, *The Deserted Village*:

> *Ill fares the land, to hast'ning ills a prey,*
> *Where wealth accumulates and men decay;*
> *Princes and lords may flourish, or may fade;*
> *A breath can make them as a breath has made;*
> *But a bold peasantry, their country's pride,*
> *When once destroyed, can never be supplied.*

One can't help thinking, however, that the Harcourts' tenants were probably happier in their neat, new homes. The Poet Laureate William Whitehead certainly thought so:

> *The careful matrons of the plain*
> *Had left their cots without a sigh*
> *Well pleased to house their little train*
> *In happier mansions, warm and dry.*

But then Whitehead was a close friend of the Harcourts.

Sometimes the former parish church, now isolated from its former congregation, was preserved for the worship of the landowner's family and servants and to serve as their mausoleum. Of 37 known deserted villages in Berkshire, in three both manor house and church survive, in two only the church, in 16 only the manor house, and in the rest, neither.

SACRIFICED FOR VICTORY

During the Second World War entire villages were evacuated for use as battle-training areas and never subsequently reoccupied.

Imber, on Salisbury Plain, was, like many English agricultural villages, declining in population. Its peak population of 440 was reached in 1851; by 1901 it was down to 261. When it was evacuated in December 1943 there were just 135 residents left. Damage and neglect made it impossible to reoccupy when hostilities ended.

Tyneham in Dorset was also cleared at the same time so that troops could train for the D-Day landings. The residents left a note pinned to the church door:

> *Please treat the church and houses with care;*
> *we have given up our homes, where many of us lived*
> *for generations, to help in the war to keep men free.*
> *We shall return one day and thank you for*
> *treating the village kindly.*

Tyneham was kept as part of a gunnery range. The church, however, is now a museum of village history and the graveyard still used for burials.

Creating the 16,000-acre Stanford battle-training area in Norfolk meant the loss of four villages and two hamlets. The parish church of St Mary at West Tofts, superbly remodelled by A.W.N. Pugin, has been carefully preserved.

Just after the war, Charlton in Gloucestershire was sacrificed to make Filton Airfield ready for the abortive Bristol Brabazon giant airliner project.

THE HAND OF MAN

At the fishing village of Hallsands in Devon the natural sea defences were eroded by dredging 650,000 tons of sand and gravel to make a navy dockyard. On 26 January 1917 a single storm swept away 29 houses. No lives were lost but the site was beyond reclamation.

Hydraulic schemes in Yorkshire, Derbyshire and Westmorland sealed the fate respectively of Timble and West End, Derwent and Ashopton, and Mardale. In County Durham whole villages were put up for sale between the 1960s and the 1980s as coal and lead mines became uneconomic. Leasingthorne was simply demolished in 1969.

A NEW FIELD FOR ARCHAEOLOGY

Interest in this neglected subject was stimulated by the six hundredth anniversary of the Black Death in 1949. In 1952 Professor Maurice Beresford founded the Deserted Medieval Village Research Group (now the Deserted Settlement Research Group) and in 1954 published his seminal work *The Lost Villages of England*. And if your interest remains piqued, bear in mind that there are also a further *30,000* hamlets and farms to be investigated....

ARE YOU GOING TO
✳ STOURBRIDGE FAIR? ✳

A medieval English fair was a commodity mega-market, luxury shopping-mall, labour exchange, amusement park and happy hunting-ground for quacks, cutpurses, pimps and prostitutes, all on an immense scale – but for a strictly limited period.

Weekly town markets dealt in the produce of their locality, usually within a six-mile radius. Fairs were *annual* events, designed for selling exotic products and basic goods in bulk, and attracting dealers from great distances.

Licensed by ancient custom or charter, fairs yielded rents from stallholders, plus the 'profits of justice' from a court of Pie Powder (from *pieds poudreux* = dusty feet), which dealt with sellers and buyers in dispute, enforced debts and punished thieves and brawlers. Offenders were tried as accused and punished immediately with fines, whipping or the stocks.

EASTWARD HO!

The largest fairs were in prosperous, densely populated eastern England, at Bedford, Scarborough and Stamford. St Ives was famed for wool, hides and cloth, Boston for wool and wine, and Yarmouth for herrings. Norwich had a fair for rushes, which were used for floor-covering and baskets, among other things.

BIG BUSINESS

The greatest fair of all, Stourbridge, was held two miles from the market-place of Cambridge on newly harvested fields, with more business done there between 24 August and 12 September than in the whole year in the city. The fair was given its charter by King John in 1211 to support a leper hospital. Among the many attractions at this medieval fair you would find:

- East Europeans selling furs and amber.

- Mediterranean traders with silks, spices, glassware, gemstones and fine weaponry.

- Sought-after English commodities including woollens leather, coal, iron and oysters.

- Local dealers trading wholesale in pots, baskets, salt, cheeses and butter.

- On the last day, before farmers reclaimed the fields, there was a horse fair.

SOLE SURVIVOR

Unusually, Stourbridge remained a major commercial event long after the Middle Ages, inspiring the 'Vanity Fair' described by John Bunyan in *The Pilgrim's Progress* (1678). Daniel Defoe, author, secret agent and serial bankrupt, visited in the 1720s and was dazzled:

> …*scarce any trades are omitted, goldsmiths, toyshops, braziers, turners, milliners, haberdashers, hatters, mercers, drapers, pewterers, china-warehouse…all trades that can be named in London; with coffee-houses, taverns, brandy-shops and eating-houses, innumerable.*

Apart from luxuries from London, Defoe would have found brass from Birmingham, steel from Sheffield, stockings from Leicester. At the centre was a square a hundred yards on each side for woollens, cottons, rugs, quilts, sacking, ticking, blankets and garments; this was known as 'the Duddery', hence 'duds'.

The second most important trade was in hops – 'there is scarce any price fixed for hops in England, till they know how they sell at Sturbridge Fair'. As hops were rarely grown north of the Trent, 'vast quantities' went back on the boats bringing woollens from the sheep-rearing and manufacturing counties.

Defoe believed the fair was 'the greatest in the…world' in terms of turnover:

> *wholesale men from…all parts of England…transact their business wholly in their pocket-books…make up their accounts, receive money chiefly in bills, and take orders: These…exceed by far the sales of goods actually brought to the fair, and delivered in kind… London wholesale men…carry back orders…for ten thousand pounds worth of goods a man…especially…those…who deal in heavy goods, as wholesale grocers, salters, brasiers, iron-merchants, wine-merchants…*

All this was made possible by the fact that the Cam still remained navigable: 'all heavy goods are brought even to the fair-field, by water carriage from London and other parts; first to the port of [King's] Lynn and then in barges up the Ouse, from the Ouse into the Cam, and…the very edge of the fair.'

SPEND, SPEND, SPEND

The fairgoers' spending was a huge cash injection into the local economy. Cambridge, although emptied by the university vacation, couldn't cope with their number so that, in Defoe's words, 'all the towns around are full; nay, the very barns and stables are turned into inns…to lodge the meaner sort of people'.

Every morning countryfolk converged with baskets of eggs, chickens, cheeses, butter and bread. And 'when the great hurry of wholesale business begins to be over, the gentry come in, from all parts of the county…for their diversion', spending freely at the goldsmiths and milliners and for the benefit of 'puppet-shows, drolls, rope-dancers and the like'.

For those university students who were still in town, Stourbridge offered a chance to acquire books and equipment. Isaac Newton bought his first copy of Euclid's *Elements* at the fair.

FUN OF THE FAIR

Defoe also noted, with innocent surprise, that 'there are sometimes no less than fifty hackney coaches, which come from London, and ply night and morning to carry the people to and from Cambridge'.

His sharp-eyed contemporary, Ned Ward, who ran a London pub, saw that the well-sprung hackney-carriages also served another purpose. Observing of the fair's patrons that 'their pretence is coming down to meet their customers; though it's plain by their Loitering, they have little else to do but to Drink, Smoke and Whore and to help support the fair in its Ancient Custom of Debauchery', Ward noted that the going rate for a strumpet and her client to hire a hackney for their transaction was one shilling and sixpence.

THE END OF THE FAIR

The great fairs were undermined by the growth of permanent shops, the improvement of roads and the advent of canals. Stourbridge hung on, however, because it was an excuse for the university to have a boozy bash with oysters. The mayor doggedly continued to proclaim its opening, but by 1931 attendance was down to five people, including two policemen to 'keep order'. Stourbridge finally gave up the ghost in 1933.

✳ WATER WORLD ✳

Stourbridge Fair has disappeared so completely from the record that encyclopaedia entries refer the reader to the industrial town of Stourbridge in Worcestershire – which has nothing to do with it. However, the area through which goods were ferried to and from the great fair, the Fens, does remain, though very much altered. In 1610, William Camden commented that the inhabitants, the 'Fenmen', were 'a kind of people according to the nature of the place where they dwell rude, uncivil and envious to all others whom they call Upland-men: who stalking high upon stilts, apply their minds to grazing, fishing and fowling.'

Fenmen, known as 'Slodgers' or Yellow Bellies (the latter either from the stomach of marsh frogs or the facings of the coats of the Lincolnshire Regiment). The poles were used to vault across dykes – a competitive sport at holiday times.

Lying west and south of the Wash, the Fens cover almost 2,500 square miles, traversed by the Great Ouse, the Nene, the Welland and the Witham. As Daniel Defoe noted in the 1720s, 'All the water of the middle part of England which does not run into the Thames or the Trent comes down into these fens.'

Even Camden conceded that the Fens had some useful resources: 'Great plenty it hath…of turf and sedge for the maintenance of fire: of reed also for to thatch their houses, yea and of alders…. But chiefly it bringeth forth exceeding store of willows.'

Surviving indefinitely in water, alder was good for building boats and jetties and made excellent charcoal. Willow yielded straight poles for stilts and for punting flat-bottomed boats, and pliable wands for weaving into baskets.

In Camden's day Fenmen had their own dramatic way of managing the landscape:

> *it is so plenteous and rank of certain fat grass and full hay that when they have mown down as much…as will serve their turns, they set fire to the rest and burn it in November, that it may come up again in greater abundance. At which time a man may see this fennish and moist tract flaming fire all over every way and wonder thereat.*

A WAKE! A WAKE!

It is no coincidence that the last significant leader of Saxon resistance to the Normans, Hereward the Wake (meaning 'the watchful one'), had his base in the Fens around Ely. The armoured Norman knight, like the modern battle tank, was best suited to open country and severely limited in mountains and marshes.

In 1071 William the Conqueror had to build a causeway to get into Hereward's hideaway. The rebellion was crushed but Hereward escaped by water and passed into legend.

SPADE WORK

Both the Romans and the Normans attempted to drain the Fens but the task was beyond them. In 1643 the Earl of Bedford commissioned the Dutch expert Cornelius Vermuyden to construct a system of drains and dykes, which became known as the Bedford Level. The main work involved digging out *by spade* the Old and New Bedford Rivers – each more than 20 miles long and 70 feet wide.

✸ NONSUCH ✸

…built with so great sumptuousness and rare workmanship, that it aspireth to the very top of ostentation for show; so as a man may think that all the skill of Architecture is in this piece of work bestowed and heaped up together…so many wonders…and works seeming to contend with Roman antiquities, that most worthily it may have and maintain still this name that it hath of Nonsuch.

WILLIAM CAMDEN, *BRITANNIA*, 1586

Nonsuch Palace, as its name implies, was intended by its builder, Henry VIII, to be beyond compare, impressing not by its size but also by its splendour. As 'statement architecture', it represented regal whim in action. The entire village of Cuddington was razed to create the site. A thousand acres of land was compulsorily purchased for a hunting park. Roads were diverted to ensure royal privacy. The foundations were built using stone from the recently dissolved and demolished Merton Priory.

Two storeys high, the palace was arranged around two interconnecting courtyards. The skyline of the palace was a forest of chimneys, turrets, pinnacles, cupolas, domes and battlements. The façade was festooned with exuberant plasterwork, plaques, portraits and panelling. The landscaped grounds were dotted with fountains, statues, columns and obelisks. There was also an archway, a pyramid, a banqueting house and the first grotto ever made in England.

PORTRAITS OF POWER

The lavish decorations were mostly the work of Italians, notably Nicolas Bellin of Modena, whose major contribution was a series of stucco reliefs to decorate the south front and the walls of the inner

Nonsuch appears to tower over the landscape, dwarfing the procession in the foreground but in fact its dimensions were fairly modest – in contrast to its exuberant decoration.

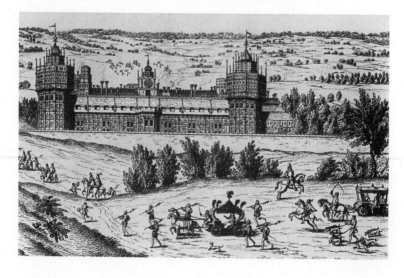

courtyard. Representing Caesars, Gods and Virtues, there may have been as many as seven or eight hundred.

By 1545, £24,536 had been lavished on the project – half as much again as the king had spent on enlarging Hampton Court. At the time of Henry's death, ten years after Nonsuch was begun, it was still unfinished. He had managed to stay there for just four days.

FROM ROYAL LODGE TO RUIN

Thereafter Nonsuch was passed from owner to owner:

- Mary Tudor, indifferent to hunting, swapped Nonsuch with the Earl of Arundel for estates in Suffolk.

- Elizabeth I came to hunt for five days in 1559, returning several times to enjoy the facilities without the expense – as was her custom.

- After Arundel died in 1579 Nonsuch passed to his son-in-law, John, Lord Lumley, who gave the gardens a makeover in the latest Italian style, the first such in England.

- By the 1590s Nonsuch was back in royal hands.

- In 1670 Charles II made over Nonsuch to his extravagant mistress, Barbara Villiers, who sold it to Lord Berkeley to pay off her gambling debts.

- Berkeley tore most of it down to use the stone for a new house at Epsom.

- By 1702 only a ruin remained.

REDISCOVERY

By the mid-twentieth century even the site of Nonsuch had been lost. It was rediscovered thanks to painstaking documentary work by a Cambridge undergraduate, Martin Biddle.

In 1959 Biddle's excavation galvanized the local community, attracting 500 volunteers and 60,000 visitors. In excavating Nonsuch, Biddle re-established the outline of the palace and also invented a new academic field – post-medieval archaeology.

✷ A SUBURBAN VERSAILLES ✷

In 1673 Sir Josiah Child, fabulously wealthy Governor of the East India Company, snapped up crumbling Tudor Wanstead House for £11,500. He then went to 'prodigious cost in planting walnut trees about his seat and making fishponds many miles in circuit'.

In 1706 Josiah's heir, Richard, commissioned royal gardener George London to transform the grounds. London had visited Louis XIV's fabulous gardens at Versailles and met their designer, Andre Le Nôtre. Contemporaries thought what London achieved at Wanstead made him 'the English Le Nôtre'.

PALLADIAN PILE

Sir Richard then employed Colen Campbell to replace the old Tudor house with a huge Palladian palace (1715–20) boasting an immense frontage of 260 feet, 70 rooms and a basement entirely for servants and services. The cost was between £200,000 and £360,000, with a further £100,000 lavished on the grounds. Inside, the décor included paintings by Hogarth and Nollekens.

Visitors included Swedish naturalist Peter Kalm, Benjamin Franklin and George III himself. During the wars against revolutionary France, Wanstead House became the residence of refugee French royalty.

RUINED BY RECKLESSNESS

By the early nineteenth century the property belonged to teenage millionairess Catherine Tylney-Long. In 1812 she married a distant

Magnificently reflected in a huge lake, Wanstead House was an uncompromising architectural statement of aristocratic arrogance – and pride did come before a fall.

relative, William Pole-Tylney-Long-Wellesley, Earl of Mornington, a nephew of the Duke of Wellington. Within ten years Mornington – drunken, unfaithful, a gambler, bully and a prodigy among wastrels – had squandered his wife's entire inheritance, forcing them to flee abroad from their creditors.

So, in 1822 the contents of Wanstead House were auctioned over 32 days, fetching £41,000. One of the fireplaces is now at George Washington's home, Mount Vernon. Selling the house itself proved fruitless, however, and in 1824 it was torn down for building stone, raising just £10,000. Catherine died, broken-hearted in 1825. Mornington lasted another 30 years as a London club bore.

Today the former site of Wanstead House is covered by Wanstead Golf Club, the former stables serving as the clubhouse. The Grotto, built in 1761 and once an ornamental boathouse, survives as a ruin, as does The Temple, a former banquet house. Aerial photographs reveal that ghostly outlines of Palladian plantings still shape the alignments of surrounding suburban streets.

WHEN BARKING RULED
✳ THE WAVES ✳

…these fishing-smacks are very useful vessels…as,
particularly in time of war, they are used as press-smacks,
running…to pick up seamen to man the navy…. At other
times…they are tenders to particular Men of War

DANIEL DEFOE, 1722

The ships described by Defoe were based in Barking, at that point a 'large market-town…chiefly inhabited by fishermen' who, by Defoe's time, had been fishing the North Sea for 400 years.

Thanks to London's insatiable appetite, over the following century Barking would become Britain's biggest fishing port and home to *the largest commercial fishing fleet in the world.*

Barking smacks could sail right up to the main fish market at Billingsgate, offering London dealers the freshest catch they could possibly get. The great fishing ports of the future, like Hull and Grimsby,

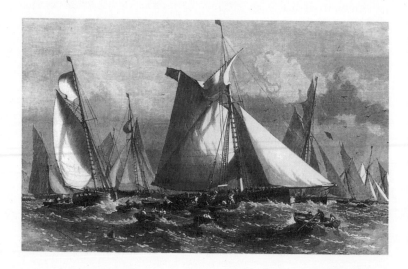

had as yet only a small, poor hinterland to sell into and, before railways, no way of reaching the major inland cities.

THE SHORT BLUE

Barking's premier fleet was known from its flag as the Short Blue. Dating from 1764, it was the creation of the shrewd Scottish Hewett family, who manned their ships with London orphans because they were cheap. The Hewetts also raised their fleet's productivity dramatically by splitting it in two. One division stayed at sea for four to eight weeks at a time, catching and packing; the other ferried out fresh supplies of ice and provisions, returning with the ready-packed fish.

By the time chips (a Belgian invention) were first paired with fish in the 1860s, the Short Blue had more than 200 vessels – and was about to move on:

- **1862** The Hewetts move the fleet headquarters to join their ship-repairing base at Gorleston on the Norfolk coast, 120 miles nearer the main fishing grounds.

- **1863** Barking's remaining fishing community is devastated by the loss of 60 men in a gale.

- **1865** The railway reaches Great Yarmouth, beyond Gorleston, and dozens of Barking families move out to rejoin the Short Blue at its new base.

- **1870** Only three smack owners remain listed in Barking.

- **1903** The last fishing smack is sold off.

The Hewetts, meanwhile, relocated to Great Yarmouth and then, in 1929, to Fleetwood in Lancashire.

Opposite *Smacks of the Short Blue fleet. The whole town prospered as Barking's poor were paid to gather winter ice from the fields to pack the fish in.*

61

✵ WHITE CITY ✵

Named after the centrepiece of the Chicago Columbian Exhibition of 1893, London's White City exhibition ground was built in 1906–1908 at Shepherd's Bush by flamboyant Hungarian impresario Imre Kiralfy.

Consisting of 20 'palaces', 120 pavilions and galleries, a scenic railway, a joy-ride, half a mile of waterways, an ornamental lake, illuminated fountains and a complete 'Irish village', the White City was first used to stage a Franco-British Exhibition which drew 8,500,000 visitors – quite overshadowing the accompanying Olympic Games.

OLYMPIC HOST

London's role as host to the fourth Olympiad in 1908 came about by default. The Games were scheduled for Rome but the eruption of Vesuvius in 1906 devastated Naples, causing the Italians to withdraw as hosts.

Britain stepped in, despite having neither a site nor a budget. A public appeal raised the cash and the world's first purpose-built Olympic facilities were rushed up in record time beside the White City exhibition area. The 'Great Stadium' included a swimming tank, pitches for hockey, rugby, football and lacrosse and an athletics track inside a banked cycling circuit. At the time, the stadium was the largest in the world, accommodating 150,000, with seating for 68,000.

A CONTROVERSIAL GAMES

The Games were the first run by experienced sports administrators – though not with the happiest results:

- At the opening ceremony the Swedes and Americans were angered to find their flags missing.

- Anglo–American friction was further aggravated by chanting for United States athletes from the sizeable contingent of American spectators, amplified by 'a new squeaking instrument of torture' – the kazoo.

- During the steeplechase heats some Americans turned up in white shorts and were made to change into regulation blue ones.

- The tug-of-war was easily won by the British team of London policemen, wearing their regulation boots, while their American opponents only had smooth-soled running shoes.

The worst incident, however, occurred during the final of the 400 metres, in which three of the four finalists were American. Accusing the Americans of colluding to impede the British favourite – a tactic thought perfectly fair in the United States – British judges scheduled a re-run in divided lanes.

The Americans refused to run again and Wyndham Halswelle was awarded the gold in the only walkover in Olympic history. Halswelle had set a new Olympic record in the semi-finals but when the American Amateur Athletic Union maintained its protest against the disqualification of the original victor, John Carpenter, Halswelle gave up athletics for good.

This way to another world: the fantastical architecture of the entrance to the White City was an appropriate expression of the showman's flair of its creator, publicist Imre Kiralfy.

MARATHON STANDARD

The London Olympics also saw the length of the marathon finally fixed. Previously run over varying distances, it was set at 26 miles, the distance from the starting-point at Windsor Castle to the finishing line at White City. Then, at the special request of the Royal Family, an additional 385 yards was tacked on so the young princes could watch the start from their bedroom. In 1921 this was retrospectively confirmed as the official marathon distance.

A CHEQUERED CAREER

Over the following 75 years the White City was used for cycling, wrestling, boxing, swimming, fly-casting, greyhound racing, floodlit rugby, clay pigeon shooting, Olympic training, speedway, American Football, the annual championships of the Amateur Athletic Association, the home fixtures of Queen's Park Rangers and the Horse of the Year Show. White City was finally demolished in 1983–4 to make way for new facilities for the BBC. The 1990 building known as White City One occupies its site.

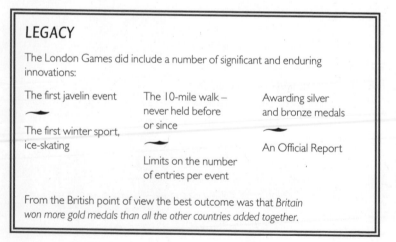

LEGACY

The London Games did include a number of significant and enduring innovations:

The first javelin event

The first winter sport, ice-skating

The 10-mile walk – never held before or since

Limits on the number of entries per event

Awarding silver and bronze medals

An Official Report

From the British point of view the best outcome was that *Britain won more gold medals than all the other countries added together.*

3
ROYALTY REMEMBERED

Soon there will be only five Kings left – the King of England,
the King of Spades, the King of Clubs, the King of Hearts
and the King of Diamonds.
FAROUK, KING OF EGYPT, 1936–52

Traditionally kings and queens formed the core of school history but they have rather fallen out of fashion, which is regrettable as the English monarchy is the oldest institution in Europe after the Papacy.

It is all too easily forgotten that when the exercise of power was intensely personal the personal qualities of the ruler *mattered*.

PARLEZ-VOUS
✷ THE KING'S ENGLISH? ✷

…first you must master their language,
their dialect, proverbs and songs…
Let them know that you know what they're saying,
let them feel that you know what they say.
RUDYARD KIPLING, *SAXON AND NORMAN*, 1911

Not many followed the deathbed advice of Kipling's imagined Norman baron to his son. For more than three centuries after the Norman Conquest no king of England spoke English as his first language.

Ruling lands on both sides of the Channel, the Norman kings spent long periods outside England. Richard the Lionheart was in England for less than six months of his ten-year reign.

William the Conqueror tried to learn English but gave up. Many of William's successors had foreign-born wives so had no domestic need for English. In fact, Henry I was the first post-Conquest king to speak English well. Most unusually he could also read and write, winning the nickname 'Beauclerk'. As William of Malmesbury recalls:

> He was early instructed in the liberal arts and so thoroughly…
> that no warlike disturbance and no pressure of business could erase
> them…. His learning, though obtained by snatches, assisted him
> much in the science of government.

In 1258 Simon de Montfort, leader of the baronial rebels against Henry III, issued his reform manifesto, the Provisions of Oxford, in English as well as in Latin, making it the first post-Conquest political document in the vernacular. Edward I chose to speak English – which fits in with his use of Parliament to support royal rule by actively endorsing his laws.

SPEAKING TO THE POINT

During the Peasants' Revolt of 1381, 14-year-old Richard II spoke to the rebels face to face, which can only have been in English. Chroniclers gave him credit for a quick tongue that saved the situation at the most critical moment of the entire revolt.

When the rebels gathered for a parley at Smithfield their leader, Wat Tyler, spoke insolently to the king and was killed by Lord Mayor William Walworth right in front of them. As the mob surged forward Richard rode right at them and declared: 'Sirs, will you shoot your king? I am your captain, follow me.'

After they had dispersed he reneged on all the promises he had made to buy time with the memorable one-liner – 'Villeins you are and villeins you shall remain.'

MAN OF MANY PARTS

It was Richard II's usurper, Henry IV, who was the first post-Conquest ruler to speak English as his mother tongue.

Henry was also the first English king known to have had a Bible in English. His library also contained books in French and Latin, and he had even studied at the prestigious University of Paris.

When the Scottish Prince James was captured en route to France for his education, Henry IV joked that they should have sent the prince to him as he could have taught him French.

As a young man Henry had fought as a crusader with the Teutonic Knights in Lithuania and travelled through Austria, Hungary, Greece, Palestine and Italy – probably able to get by with French and Latin alone.

LINGUISTICALLY CHALLENGED

Shakespeare has great fun showing Henry IV's son and heir, Henry V, battling manfully with French to woo his queen, Catherine of Valois.

> *I will tell thee in French, which I am sure will hang upon my tongue like a new-married wife about her husband's neck, hardly to be shook off.... It is as easy for me, Kate, to conquer the kingdom as to speak so much more French. I shall never move thee in French, unless it be to laugh at me.*
> HENRY V IN *THE LIFE OF HENRY THE FIFTH*, ACT 5 SCENE 2

But it was also Henry V who first ordered government documents to be written in English. Taking this royal cue, London brewers drafted their ordinances in English – 'our mother tongue…[which]…hath in modern days begun to be honourably enlarged…and our most excellent lord, King Henry V, hath procured the common idiom…to be commended by the exercise of writing.' The English delegation to the Council of Constance declared language to be 'the most sure and positive sign and essence of a nation in divine and human law'.

SPEECHMAKING SUPERSTAR

I am more afraid of making a fault in my Latin than of the Kings of Spain, France, Scotland, the whole house of Guise and all of their confederates.
ELIZABETH I, OF HERSELF

Henry VIII was quite outshone by his brilliant daughter, Elizabeth I, who was famed for her impromptu speeches, fluency in other languages and witticisms:

At the age of *twelve* she gave him a New Year's Day present of the *Prayers and Meditations* of her stepmother Katherine Parr, which she had translated into Latin, French and Italian.

Visiting the University of Cambridge, the queen was asked to say a sentence in Latin and gave an impromptu address of 800 words.

Visiting Oxford, Elizabeth broke off her Latin speech to ask in English for a chair for her most trusted counsellor, the ageing Lord Burleigh, then picked up in Latin precisely where she had left off. She was making a point. The day before she had rebuked the university orator for learning his over-long speech of welcome parrot-fashion and not being able to edit it down.

In 1597 the queen gave an insolent Polish ambassador an off-the-cuff tongue-lashing in Latin that neither he nor her courtiers ever forgot.

Elizabeth read Greek daily, understood Spanish and was still translating philosophical works from Latin in her sixties.

Henry VII must have found his family's Welsh ancestry useful when he was in exile in Brittany as Welsh and Breton are mutually comprehensible. His son, Henry VIII, spoke French and some Italian and was an accomplished scholar in Latin, writing a learned refutation of the teachings of Luther that led the Pope to award him the title of 'Defender of the Faith'. Married to Katherine of Aragon for more than 20 years, the king was also fluent in Spanish.

PILLOW TALK

Linguistically mixed marriages remained the norm for English royalty:

Elizabeth's successor, James VI and I, was married to Anne of Denmark. A frustrated academic, with a complete mastery of Latin, Greek and French, he wrote poetry in both English and Scots, a treatise on government and counterblasts against witchcraft and tobacco.

~

Charles I could presumably converse with his French wife in her own language but, like his father, never threw off his strong Scottish accent or his stammer.

~

Charles II spent years of exile in France and the Netherlands, as well as having a Portuguese wife, so his linguistic credentials were more than respectable.

~

James II's second wife was Italian.

~

William III was a Dutchman married to James II's English daughter, Mary.

Queen Anne married a Danish prince who habitually spoke French.

~

German George I did have a German wife but kept her locked away for most of her life and never himself bothered to learn English.

~

George II and his spouse were both German-speakers. The king, however, spoke English fluently from childhood, although with a marked guttural accent. His clever wife, Caroline of Anspach, also became fluent in English but corresponded in French.

~

George III gloried in his Englishness but spoke French and German well.

~

Queen Victoria and her husband, Prince Albert habitually spoke German between themselves. Long after Albert's death Victoria favoured ministers and officials who could converse with her in German.

A PRINCIPLED PRINCE

Prince Charles is the first ever Prince of Wales to attempt to learn to speak Welsh.

ROYAL AMBASSADOR

In an age when monarchs continued to play a personal part in foreign policy, a command of languages still mattered. Edward VII may not have been the real architect of the *rapprochement* between Britain and France that led to the 'Entente Cordiale' of 1904, but his ability to charm the French public in their own language was certainly of great assistance.

�֍ PHILIP, KING OF ENGLAND ✶

Determined to restore England to the Roman faith, Mary Tudor tried to make the restoration permanent by marrying the most powerful Catholic king, Philip II of Spain.

The House of Commons begged her not to, fearing England would become a mere province of the Habsburg Empire, which already covered half of western Europe and much of South America.

Mary and Philip were married in Winchester Cathedral in July 1554. The English Parliament, however, successfully stalled requests for Philip's coronation.

At Mary's insistence Philip was, although uncrowned, given the title of king and it was ordered that all official documents and Acts of Parliament were to be issued and dated in their joint names. On coins his likeness appeared with hers, face to face. Jointly their style was the longest ever used by a British sovereign:

> *Philip and Mary, by the Grace of God, King and Queen of*
> *England and France, Naples, Jerusalem and Ireland,*
> *Defenders of the Faith, Princes of Spain and Sicily, Archdukes*
> *of Austria, Dukes of Milan, Burgundy and Brabant, Count*
> *and Countess of Flanders, Habsburg and Tyrol.*

(Apparently the immense South American assets counted for nothing in terms of prestige.)

Mary fell deeply in love with Philip. Philip, 11 years her junior, found her repellent. Mary was short-sighted, suffered from severe headaches and gave off a terrible smell from her nose, probably as a result of a bone infection.

Philip nevertheless stuck it out for 14 months before returning to Spain. He came back in 1557 and was greeted joyfully at Greenwich. Mary readily agreed to support his current war against France. Philip then left in July, never to return. As a result of the war England lost Calais, its last foothold on mainland France, leading Mary to say: 'When I am dead and opened you shall find "Calais" lying in my heart.'

Philip has the unique distinction of being the only king consort in English history. Expressing 'a reasonable regret' at Mary's death in 1558, he believed he still had a claim on the English throne. Thirty years later Philip finally got around to sending an 'Invincible Armada' to make this claim good. But, according to the victory medal struck for English Armada veterans, 'God blew and they were scattered.'

Come on, you Dons! A contemporary woodcut emphasizes English preparations against a Spanish landing – batteries of artillery, close-packed phalanxes of pikemen and beacon-towers to signal the invaders' arrival. Appropriately, a figure representing the wind is shown bottom left – as so often, it was the weather that actually proved decisive.

QUEEN'S COUNSELLORS

Not the least of Elizabeth I's many talents was the ability to command devoted service from remarkably talented men, and her court was well known for gallants, poets, statesmen and buccaneers. Cecil, Sydney, Spenser, Raleigh, Drake and Hawkins achieved some fame but others, less well known, were no less important.

THE QUEEN'S MAGUS

John Dee traced his descent from Welsh royalty and was a Fellow of Trinity College, Cambridge at 19. Living past 80, he lectured variously in Paris, Antwerp, Louvain, Venice, Prague and Poland, becoming an expert in fields as diverse as stage-effects and secret codes.

'Dr Dee' made himself useful in several ways. For example, he chose the auspicious date for Elizabeth's coronation. When a wax doll of the queen was found stuck with pins, Dr Dee exorcized the intended evil. And when a comet seemed to portend some disaster, the queen sat patiently through Dee's briefing on its implications.

Settling at Mortlake, Dee accumulated 3,000 books and 1,000 manuscripts, the greatest private library in England. Dee devoted his later life to alchemy and communicating with spirits but still managed to sire 11 children after the age of 50. Dee also advocated the creation of what he was the first to name – 'the British Empire'.

THE DANCING CHANCELLOR

Sir Christopher Hatton caught the queen's eye with his grace as a dancer but rose to become Captain of her bodyguard and eventually Lord Chancellor.

Hatton persuaded the queen's secretary, Davison, to send off the warrant for the execution of Mary, Queen of Scots. Elizabeth vented her rage on the luckless Davison. Hatton was pleased to have removed a long-standing focus for conspiracies against the queen.

Hatton served the queen crucially by managing the debates of the House of Commons with finesse and by collaborating with Archbishop Whitgift to enforce uniformity of worship in the newly established Church of England.

A favourite of the queen for 30 years, Hatton was cosseted on his death-bed by Elizabeth in person, feeding him broth from her own hand. Hatton died a Knight of the Garter and Chancellor of the University of Oxford and was buried in St Paul's.

London's jewelry district, Hatton Garden, occupies the site of his London home, while Hatton's country house at Holdenby, Northamptonshire, was thought the greatest building of its time. Built to entertain the queen, it wrecked Hatton's finances irretrievably. Elizabeth never went there.

THE MONEY MAN

Sir Thomas Gresham, the queen's financial wizard, persuaded her to restore the purity of English coinage and dramatically cut her debts by borrowing from London merchants, rather than foreigners. He also smuggled huge quantities of cash out of the Netherlands in bales of pepper and suits of armour, as well as ammunition disguised as 'velvets'.

Gresham accumulated five country houses, established a pioneering paper mill, made an immense fortune and gave London its first purpose-built bourse and shopping mall, the Royal Exchange. He also founded Gresham College where free public lectures were given – and still are.

THE TURNCOAT

Gresham's successor as Elizabeth's financial fixer was Sir Horatio Palavicino, a Genoese adventurer appointed by Mary Tudor to collect papal taxes. When Mary died he turned Protestant and kept the taxes he had collected to found his own fortune. As a result, Palavicino accumulated 8,000 acres of land in three counties and once tried to corner the world's entire supply of pepper.

His extensive network of agents abroad, however, made him an invaluable source of intelligence for the secret service.

Palavicino once made a loan of £29,000 to the queen – and got back £41,000 in interest alone. The outstanding principal remained a matter of contention for years.

Palavicino's heir squandered his entire fortune and died in debtors' prison.

THE TRUSTED COUSIN

Henry Carey, Baron Hunsdon, was an expert jouster and a Garter Knight and Privy Councillor before he was 30, although he remained a rough diamond, loathed by courtiers and loved by soldiers.

When the last aristocratic uprising broke out in 1569, Hunsdon smashed it by leading 1,500 men to victory over a force twice their number. At the time of the Armada, it was Hunsdon who commanded the queen's personal bodyguard.

Although the queen's meanness often forced Hunsdon to pay his men out of his own pocket, she did personally pay for his funeral. Hunsdon's widow raised the largest and most extravagant tomb in Westminster Abbey over his grave, 36 feet high.

THE FATED PHYSICIAN

Rodrigo Lopez, a Portuguese Jew, became personal physician to the queen's favourite, the Earl of Leicester, and in 1586 to the queen herself.

However, Lopez made an enemy of her new favourite, the Earl of Essex, by refusing to spy for him. Later he was approached by agents of Philip II with a huge bribe to poison the queen. Lopez foolishly failed to return a jewel sent as a down payment. The Privy Council soon became aware of the plot. Lopez was arrested and tried by a special commission chaired by ... Essex.

Although no direct evidence could be brought against him, he was sentenced to be hanged, drawn and quartered. Normally the property of traitors was forfeit. Unusually, Elizabeth allowed Lopez's family to keep most of his and paid for his son's school fees.

The luckless Lopez was almost certainly the inspiration for Shakespeare's Shylock and also appeared in Marlowe's *Dr Faustus* as well as in plays by Dekker, Middleton and Taylor.

Elizabeth is said to have worn the jewel bribe at her waist for the rest of her life.

MASQUE OF MONARCHY

The 'age of Shakespeare' is revered for a new art form – theatre. But for the elite of the day the catchpenny afternoon amusements of squalid Southwark were quite overshadowed by the courtly masque in which royalty itself took the lead.

While the commercial theatre operated with minimal scenery and without artificial lighting, the masque, combining mime, music, verse and dance, and performed in extravagant costumes with elaborate stage-effects, was an altogether more dazzling experience.

The masque evolved out of Tudor 'disguisings' when courtiers, wearing outlandish costumes and masks, welcomed esteemed guests with fanfares, songs, dances and flowery, flattering speeches. As an artistic form, the masque was seminal in introducing the proscenium arch, the front curtain and numerous scenic effects depending on artificial lighting and an understanding of perspective.

JONSON AND JONES

It was Ben Jonson, as scriptwriter, who first coined the term 'masque'. His collaborator was royal architect Inigo Jones, who had travelled in Italy and learned first hand the latest styles of lighting, staging and costume design.

Their first production, presented on Twelfth Night, 1605, was *The Masque of Blackness*. Queen Anne of Denmark herself played the leading role, attended by 11 court ladies, made up as 'Ethiopians'. The king was presented with fans symbolizing his divinely ordained authority, his uniting of England and Scotland to create the new empire of Great Britain and his wisdom in ending the long war with Spain. These self-congratulatory themes were to be often repeated in subsequent masques.

PRINCELY PRODUCTIONS

The masque devised for the investiture of Henry as Prince of Wales in 1610 had an Arthurian theme – Arthur being both an embodiment of kingly virtue and valour and supposedly of Welsh origin. Henry

EXTRAVAGANZA

Masques were staggeringly expensive to mount, even by the standards of the spendthrift Stuart court:

For *Oberon* the costumes alone cost more than £1,400 – enough to build a parish church. (Jones got just £16 for designing them.)

Mounted only once or twice, masques demanded complex stage machinery, costumes of silk and taffeta shot through with silver and gold, orchestras of 50 musicians or more, a small army of carpenters, painters, seamstresses and stagehands, and hundreds of torches and fine wax candles for illumination and lighting effects.

Charles I decided to cut out masques as part of an economy drive but reinstated them after five years, capping the budget at £1,400 and ordering courtiers to pay for their own costumes – the most expensive component.

This wanton waste appalled the Puritan element in a kingdom still pestered with beggars and the very real threat of famine.

himself starred in the debut performance. The following year's masque featured Henry as *Oberon
the Fairy Prince*.

THE COST OF CRITICISM

In 1632 Queen Henrietta Maria herself
appeared on stage in a speaking part.
Shortly afterwards Puritan pamphleteer
William Prynne published a long diatribe
against the theatre, including masques,
which he blasted as a shadow representa-
tion of the Mass.

*Inigo Jones's costume design for a 'Watery Spirit'.
Characters in the masque invariably represented mythic or
symbolic figures, all too appropriately unreal in relation to the self-
deluding message of national unity and contentment under Stuart rule.*

Prynne's index reference to 'Women actors, Notorious whores' was
taken as a not-so-veiled reference to the queen herself. Prynne was
fined £500, pilloried, had both ears cut off and was sent to the Tower of
London for life. He was released in 1640, when Parliament finally
reassembled after an interval of 11 years.

THEATRE OF DELUSION

Under Charles I the element of spectacle, especially the dances in
which the royal couple themselves took part, came to overshadow the
literary content, causing Jonson to resign in disgust.

As the Stuart monarchy edged blindly towards disaster, its celebrations proclaimed with sublime self-delusion the perfection of its
governance. *Albion's Triumph* was followed by *British Heaven* and
Victorious Britain. The last masque, performed as crisis loomed with

the enforced recall of a vengeful Parliament, assured their majesties in its final song that:

> All that are harsh, all that are rude,
> Are by your harmony subdued…

Alas, not so.

THE GLORIOUS INVASION
✸ OF 1688 ✸

William III's landfall in 1688 and the manoeuvrings that made him co-sovereign with his English wife, Mary, are known as the 'Glorious Revolution'.

The underlying issue of the civil wars was at last settled with the monarchy's acceptance of the supremacy of Parliament. The revolution was glorious because it was bloodless – in England. It need not have been so.

WHO WANTED WHAT?

William meant business – but nobody can be sure what business he meant. He was invited by aristocratic conspirators to make James II, his father-in-law, stop trying to promote Catholicism and royal absolutism. However, William's main aim was to bring England into his coalition to protect his native Netherlands from France. The letter of invitation he received made no mention of overthrowing his father-in-law and William made no proclamation of intending to do so.

'PROTESTANT WIND'

William's expeditionary force, a Dutch army with contingents of Danes, Germans, Russians and Finns, was carried in 50 men-of-war and 500 troop transports. William waited at sea for two days – an uncomfortable and risky option in winter – so that he could land on

5 November, the anniversary of the treasonous Catholic Gunpowder Plot, a date pregnant with meaning for Protestant Englishmen. They hailed a 'Protestant Wind' which had brought them a saviour from Popery while keeping their own, much larger, fleet penned in the Thames.

MARCH TO POWER

After landing on the Devon coast, William took possession of Exeter. James, with a much larger army, moved at a leisurely pace until detained at Winchester for two days with a violent nosebleed. The delay proved decisive in giving his generals time to defect.

William advanced steadily on London, accumulating support. James, deserted by his army, fled, vacating the throne.

William entered London to claim a capital from which English troops were withdrawn as a precaution against an accidental clash of arms. William and Mary were jointly offered the throne and jointly crowned. William even got Parliament to pay for the costs of the invasion.

'My Husband and I'. The crown was actually offered to Mary in recognition of her royal bloodline but she refused to accept it unless she could reign in partnership with her husband. To emphasize this, both are shown wielding sceptres as symbols of authority.

GOD SAVE GREAT GEORGE
✳ OUR KING ✳

The name and notion of a national anthem are both British inventions and Britain's is the oldest – although it has never been formally endorsed, either by royal proclamation or Act of Parliament.

AUTHOR UNKNOWN

Authorship of the anthem is uncertain and variously attributed to the appropriately named Dr John Bull (died 1628), Thomas Ravenscroft (1633), Henry Purcell (1695) and Henry Carey (1743), composer of 'Sally in Our Alley'. It first appeared in print in *Harmonia Anglicana* in 1742, where its authorship is unhelpfully credited to the prolific 'Anon.'.

The anthem became suddenly popular in September 1745, when it was sung after a performance at Drury Lane as Bonnie Prince Charlie's army seemed to threaten London, throwing the capital into alternate bouts of panic and patriotism. The words soon appeared in print in the *Gentleman's Magazine*, the first line being 'God save great George our King' – the George in question being George II (reigned 1727–60).

Thomas Arne, composer of *Rule, Britannia!*, arranged the anthem for performance at Drury Lane and the learned musicologist Dr Charles Burney did the same for Covent Garden.

NINE VERSES

A near-original text, as reproduced in *The Aviary: or, Magazine of British Melody* of about 1750 runs to nine verses. The fourth is very specific about the threat of the Jacobite rebellion:

NAVY CODE

The phrase 'God Save the King' is found in Miles Coverdale's 1535 translation of the Bible and passed into use as a naval watchword, with the response 'Long to reign over us'.

> *Oh! Grant that Marshal Wade*
> *May, by thy mighty Aid,*
> > *Victory bring:*
> *May he Sedition hush,*
> *And like a Torrent rush*
> *Rebellious Scots to crush,*
> > *God save the King.*

Verse five confounds the Pope, the French and the Spanish, and verse six excoriates,

> *Priests with bald-headed Pates,*
> *Of the French King.*

Verse seven renews praise for 'valiant Marshal Wade', verse eight calls on the royal family to 'multiply' and verse nine urges a loyal toast and concludes with a prayer, singularly fitting for a commercial nation, that 'Heavens grant the Wars to cease, That trading may encrease'.

Marshal Wade (1673–1748) foiled a Jacobite rising in the West Country in 1715, became MP for Bath and built a network of military roads to police the Highlands. As Commander-in-Chief at 72 he proved ineffectual against Bonnie Prince Charlie and retired in favour of George II's brutish son, 'Butcher' Cumberland.

WELL-TRAVELLED TUNE

In 1832 the American Samuel F. Smith took the tune for his composition *My Country, 'Tis of Thee*, which became second in popularity only to *The Star-Spangled Banner*. The tune was also adopted for the German national anthem *Heil dir in Siegerkranz – Hail to Thee in Victor's Garlands* – until replaced by the Deutschlandlied in 1922.

Although nowadays only the first, and sometimes the third verses of the original are sung, Marshal Wade still enjoys the unusual distinction of being one of the few individuals – indeed, perhaps the only one – to be named in a national anthem.

✳ A PEOPLE'S PRINCESS ✳

Caroline of Brunswick-Wolfenbüttel was unstuffy, kind-hearted, boisterous and none too fond of washing. In 1795, aged 27, she was chosen to marry her reprobate cousin, George, Prince of Wales. The prince agreed on condition his debts of £630,000 were paid and his income doubled.

At the first meeting of bride and groom the prince turned to his companion and said: 'Harris, I am feeling faint. Fetch me a brandy.'

The bridegroom allegedly spent his wedding night in the fireplace, dead drunk. Caroline nevertheless conceived and gave birth to a daughter, Charlotte, by which time the prince had formally separated from her.

SEPARATE LIVES

Caroline set up house in Blackheath, entertaining a stream of male visitors. A 'Delicate Investigation' in 1806 found much evidence of impropriety but none of adultery.

In 1811 the prince became Regent as his father, George III, descended into madness. He immediately denied Charlotte access to her own daughter, and so in 1813 Caroline left to live abroad, touring the Continent with a bizarre assortment of hangers-on. Princess Charlotte grew up only to die in 1817 in childbirth after two miscarriages and a labour of 50 hours. She was buried with her stillborn son beneath a superb memorial in St George's Chapel, Windsor.

THE WOMAN WHO WOULD BE QUEEN

When George III died in 1820 the Regent, now George IV, offered Caroline £50,000 a year provided she stayed away. Caroline rejected the offer indignantly and, on landing in England was received with great warmth by the public, who despised her self-indulgent, wastrel husband.

The king then tried to have Parliament depose her and dissolve his marriage. As he did so Caroline was bombarded with 'addresses of sympathy'. When the king's 'Bill of Pains and Penalties' was withdrawn there were three days of public rejoicing.

FATAL ENCOUNTER

But when Caroline turned up for George's coronation she was denied access by a bodyguard of bareknuckle boxers hired for the occasion.

This humiliation proved literally fatal and three weeks later Caroline was dead. News of Napoleon's death reached London at virtually the same time. On being informed that 'Your bitterest enemy is dead,' the king replied: 'Is she, by God?'

In accordance with Caroline's request, her body was to be taken back to Brunswick for burial. Well-wishers turned out all the way along the route to express their respect for a woman wronged.

Little and large. The voluptuous, if compact, Princess Caroline takes a stroll with her 'constant companion' Count Bartolomeo Bergami, whose family ran her household.

4

THE BLAST OF WAR

This fortress built by Nature for herself,
Against infection and the hand of war
WILLIAM SHAKESPEARE, *RICHARD II*

When England hasn't actually been at war it has been either recovering from one or preparing for the next.

- During the 'Second Hundred Years War' which ended in 1815, England went to war 11 times for a total of 56 years.

- The eighteenth century saw the birth of the Industrial Revolution – but far more men served in the armed forces or the militia than ever saw the inside of a factory.

✷ ENGLAND'S BIGGEST BATTLE ✷

Schools tend not to 'do' the Wars of the Roses any more, which is probably why many people wouldn't know when, where or why what was quite probably Britain's biggest, bloodiest battle was fought.

Five years of see-saw skirmishing for the crown between the rival houses of Lancaster and York reached a peak in 1460. In July of that year the Yorkists won at Northampton, capturing hapless King Henry VI, but were defeated at Wakefield in December.

In February 1461 it was the Yorkists turn to win again, at Mortimer's Cross in Herefordshire. Spurred by this victory, 18-year-old Edward, Earl of March, set off for London to declare himself king.

A fortnight after Mortimer's Cross the two sides clashed at St Albans. The Lancastrians rescued Henry VI but couldn't stop Edward getting to London and being recognized as the rightful king. They retreated northwards to regroup with Edward in pursuit.

BATTLE FOR THE BRIDGE

The decisive confrontation took place 15 miles from York, where Henry VI took refuge. The Lancastrian army spread itself between the villages of Towton and Saxton, north of the River Aire. They may have numbered 40,000 but their commander, the Duke of Somerset, was only 24. Edward, although even younger, had an experienced veteran, Lord Fauconberg, as deputy, and an almost equal force, of 36,000. Modern scholars doubt these numbers and assume each side had about 20,000 men.

On 28 March, in driving sleet, there was a skirmish for a bridge over the Aire. Mounted Yorkist archers crossed the river through unguarded shallows, took the Lancastrians off guard and inflicted significant casualties.

SUNDAY SLAUGHTER IN SNOW

The main engagement took place the next day, 29 March, Palm Sunday. To complicate matters the fight would, despite the date, take place in a blinding snowstorm.

At about nine o'clock in the morning the wind suddenly veered to blow in the Yorkists' favour and into faces of the Lancastrians.

Wily Fauconberg pushed his archers forward, ordering them to fire a single volley to provoke the Lancastrians and immediately fall back. Shooting with the wind the Yorkist archers gained extra range but the Lancastrians' return fire fell short by 40 yards. Fauconberg then ordered his archers to gather up the Lancastrians' wasted arrows and return them to their owners.

COLD COMFORT

The two main bodies then clashed in savage fighting lasting fully ten hours. Had the battle been in summer the combatants, encased in up to 60 pounds of armour and padding, would have been felled by heat exhaustion. As it was, the cold may have dulled the pain of wounds and helped blood coagulate.

By dusk it seemed the Yorkists must yield as Edward's army was gradually pushed back towards the river. Then, facing defeat, they heard the Duke of Norfolk arriving with a long-expected force of fresh troops. Panic seized the Lancastrians. They broke and fled.

MASSACRE

According to the Chronicler of Croyland Abbey, the Yorkists pursued and gave no quarter, 'cutting down the fugitives, just like so many sheep for the slaughter…the blood of the slain, mingling with the snow…ran down in the furrows and ditches…'.

The rout became a massacre, leaving a carpet of corpses almost half a mile wide and six miles long. Five Lancastrian peers were killed in the battle and two more were executed soon after. The political opposition to the Yorkists had been literally annihilated.

Edward IV could now look forward to organizing his coronation. Henry VI fled to a decade of exile in Scotland.

DEATH TOLL

It has been claimed that 28,000 men died at Towton, of whom 20,000 were Lancastrian. If so, that would represent a third of all the fatalities produced in 30 years of warfare. Modern sceptics put the death toll at about 10,000, slightly less than those of the civil war battles of Marston Moor (1644) and Worcester (1651).

1066 AND ALL THE OTHERS

1066, as we all know, was the last time England was invaded. Or was it?

1100s Henry of Anjou, repeatedly invaded England during the civil war between his mother, Matilda, and King Stephen until succeeding Stephen as Henry II.

1213 A planned French invasion was thwarted at sea but the future Louis VIII of France did become – if temporarily – a rival ruler to King John.

1338 The French burned Southampton as a foretaste of full-scale invasion but had their fleet destroyed in 1340 at the Battle of Sluys.

1360 The French raided and destroyed Winchelsea.

1400 French troops assisted the uprising of Owen Glendower in Wales.

1485 Henry, Duke of Richmond, landed at Milford Haven with 2,000 men, including foreign troops, to claim the crown as Henry VII.

1545 The French seized the Isle of Wight for 24 hours but were chased away before they could land troops on the mainland.

1778 American privateer John Paul Jones raided Whitehaven and destroyed the shore battery.

1781 A French force seized St Helier, Jersey, but was forced to surrender by the local garrison and militia.

1797 1,400 French troops failed to reach Bristol but landed at Fishguard in Wales, got drunk and were surrendered by their American commander because it was 'unnecessary to attempt any military operations as they would only tend to bloodshed'.

Floating fortress, a French secret weapon supposedly built for an invasion of Britain in 1798. A British Admiral reassured the House of Lords – 'I do not say they cannot come, my Lords, I only say they cannot come by sea.'

Battle of the Roses. An imaginative re-creation of Towton emphasizes close-packed hand-to-hand fighting, but the preliminary archery duel and culminating pursuit were to prove decisive in settling the outcome.

Perhaps archaeology will settle the matter one day. Certainly the bodies of young men have been found all over the battlefield, in Saxton churchyard, beside the main road and even in the cellars of nearby Towton Hall.

A PEACEFUL WAR?

Perhaps the real significance of Towton was that although it was decisive for the combatants, the rest of the population could virtually ignore it. As a detached observer, the Burgundian diplomat Philip de Commynes, noted:

> *out of all the countries which I have personally known, England is*
> *the one where public affairs are best conducted and regulated with*
> *the least violence to the people. There neither the countryside nor*
> *the people are destroyed, nor are buildings burned or demolished.*
> *Disaster and misfortune fall only on those who make war,*
> *the soldiers and the nobles.*

Modern scholarship confirms this judgment. While the toffs and the toughs chased, battered and murdered each other, the peasantry could follow their ploughs and tend their flocks unmolested.

Despite long periods of truce, France was horribly devastated by the Hundred Years War. During the Wars of the Roses, by contrast, no English cities were sacked, no regions despoiled. Indeed, the vast mass of the population enjoyed a prosperity that increased, if modestly, at least as steadily as the uncertainties of harvest and plague allowed.

Perhaps Britain's bloodiest battle is rightfully forgotten.

�֍ CIVIL WAR AND CIVILIZATION �֍

Unlike the Wars of the Roses, the civil wars of the 1640s *did* involve the sacking of towns and large-scale killings of non-combatants.

These wars militarized a profoundly civilian society. By 1644 perhaps 150,000 men were under arms, one in eight of all adult males. Total fatalities for the wars, military and civilian, were around 100,000. The fighting, ended by the abolition of monarchy in 1649, was followed by a decade of social experiment. The Restoration of monarchy in 1660 brought a decade of reaction.

THE ROYAL SOCIETY

Many intellectuals abandoned London and kept a low profile. In Oxford, however, a group with interests in science met informally at Wadham College to read papers and conduct experiments. After the Restoration they convened at Gresham College, London, and in 1662

EXPERIMENTS, NOVELTIES, INVENTIONS & INNOVATIONS

Histories of the Civil War period inevitably focus on battles and politics, neglecting other significant events and developments.

SOCIETY

The massive disruption of familiar routines and uprooting of hundreds of thousands of individuals led to some surprising social innovations:

1649 The first employment agency, known as the 'Office of Entries'.

1650 The first marriage bureau, the 'Office of Addresses and Encounters'.

1657 The first classified advertisements, categorized under Shipping, Properties for Sale and To Let, Physicians, Artificers, Lost and Stolen (including people!), Stage Coaches and Carriers.

1659 The first debating club, the Rota, voted on motions using a ballot box.

None of these lasted more than a few months.

DOING BUSINESS

Trade and industry were also taking great strides forward:

1646 The first printed advertisements appear in the *Perfect Diurnall*.

1646 Jeremiah Rich introduces a workable system of shorthand writing.

1650s Steel-springed coaches give a much smoother ride. Post-horns are blown from coaches to claim right of way.

1657 Col. Blount's 'Waywiser', the first mileometer, is fitted to a London coach.

1658 The first shares – in the East India Company – are traded.

1659 The first cheque is written, for £10.

1662 Parliament authorizes the charging of tolls to pay for road repairs.

1670 A regular coach service links Oxford and London.

LIFESTYLE

There were some notable improvements in day-to-day life:

1644 Archaeologists excavating a latrine at Dudley Castle, Staffordshire in 1986 discovered five condoms which they dated to its siege. Made of fish and animal guts, they were probably brought back from France.

1648 The first British barometer was made in London by Theodor Haak, a translator by profession.

1649 A letter addressed to Sir Ralph Verney asks him to buy 'little brushes for making clean of the teeth' in Paris.

1656 To evade the ban on plays, courtier William Davenant puts on a five-act opera, *The Siege of Rhodes*, in a private performance at Clerkenwell. This is the first stage production in England to feature movable scenery and an actress.

1658 Pendulum clock is introduced by Ahasuerus Fromanteel from the Netherlands.

1661 Charles II, returning from exile, introduces competitive yacht-racing and ice skating.

1663 Busy bureaucrat Samuel Pepys is given a 'silver reservoir pen'.

1666 Samuel Pepys has the first glass-fronted bookcases made.

RELIGION
Parliament, dominated by Puritans, closed down theatres, banned animal-baiting, football and folk-dancing, and prohibited the celebration of Christmas. The breakdown of the authority of the Church of England led to an upsurge in unorthodox religious life:

1648 George Fox founds the Society of Friends, derisively known as 'Quakers'. In 1651 Fox became the first known conscientious objector when he was imprisoned for refusing to join the parliamentary army.

1649 'Diggers' attempt to create a Utopian community by cultivating land at St George's Hill, Weybridge.

1652 The first Unitarian congregation is founded.

1657 The Rector of Tamworth, Staffordshire, is the first to use the title 'Reverend'.

ARMY AND NAVY
Innovations in warfare were institutional rather than technological.

1643, 1650, 1653 The first medals for gallantry, for a campaign and for meritorious service are awarded.

1642, 1650, 1656, 1659 Senior regiments of the Household Division are established: the Scots Guards; the Blues & Royals and the Coldstream Guards; the Grenadiers; the Life Guards.

1647 The navy adopts a standardized flag code.

1650s Sailors are issued with a daily rum ration.

Bookplate of Samuel Pepys. An enthusiastic bibliophile, Pepys amassed a library of 3,000 volumes, meticulously catalogued and uniformly bound. Childless, he bequeathed them to his alma mater, Magdalene College, Cambridge.

were chartered as the Royal Society, which today is the oldest continuously existing scientific society in the world. In 1665 the Society began to publish Britain's first learned journal, the *Acta Philosophica*. Robert Hooke, who organized the Society's experiments, was the first paid professional scientist; his *Micrographia* (also 1665) showed for the first time what could be seen with the aid of a microscope.

A flea and a louse as depicted in Hooke's Micrographia. *Samuel Pepys thought it 'the most ingenious book I ever read in my life'. As President of the Royal Society, Pepys later gave the go-ahead for the printing of Isaac Newton's* Principia.

✵ SIGN OF A HERO ✵

If you are a regular pub-goer the name Marquis of Granby might sound vaguely familiar. But who was he?

John Manners, Marquis of Granby was a Member of Parliament at 20 and a colonel at 24. Leading heavy cavalry at the Battle of Warburg in 1760, Granby pressed fearlessly forward, losing both his hat and his wig – so his bald head invariably figures prominently on the signs of the many pubs named after him.

The Marquis eventually became Commander-in-Chief of the British Army. He was painted by Sir Joshua Reynolds no less than twelve times and had a town in Massachusetts named in his honour.

London's West End alone has at least four Marquis of Granby pubs and others are scattered from Norfolk to Staffordshire, from Yorkshire to Surrey. They are especially thick on the ground in the Marquis's home county, Leicestershire, and in garrison towns like Colchester.

One reason for these tributes is his well-deserved reputation as a hero. Another is the fact that men who served under him received a personal gratuity when they were discharged through injury or age. What could be more natural than so many should fulfil an old soldier's dream and buy a pub – naming it after the man who made it possible.

Ironically, there was no tranquil old age for Granby. His later years were clouded by unmerited political attacks and harassment by his creditors. He died £37,000 in debt, not yet 50.

FORTUNES OF WAR

Granby won fame but died hugely in debt, a fate shared by many brothers-in-arms. Numerous naval heroes, by contrast, managed to gain fame and fortune.

While the officer class of the army was for centuries dominated by aristocratic privilege, the Royal Navy offered a career where competence counted for more than connections.

Life in the army could whittle away a fortune with the pressure to purchase promotions, drink heavily and gamble recklessly. The navy in wartime offered the possibility of fabulous wealth.

Enemy ships taken intact yielded a share of prize money to every member of the crew responsible for their capture. A captain on £200 a year might collect £40,000 – two centuries' pay!

The greatest prize ever taken was by Lt Herbert Sawyer, commanding the frigate *Active*, a mere 28-gunner, who seized the Spanish treasure-ship *Hermione* off Cádiz in 1762 with £544,000 in cash and bullion aboard. Almost within sight of home, the luckless captain of the *Hermione* didn't even know that Spain and Britain were at war.

Sawyer's share of the prize amounted to £65,053 13s. 9d. To his great credit, rather than opting for ease ashore, Sawyer served for another 33 years, rising to the position of Admiral.

As the Navy never managed to build as many ships as it needed, prizes were vital to its success and during the Napoleonic Wars accounted for more than a quarter of the entire fleet.

APART FROM TRAFALGAR AND ✳ WATERLOO... ✳

It is quite possible to read Jane Austen's novels without realizing that Britain was at war with France for the entire adult lifetime of all the main characters. For Austen's young ladies, the presence of officers suggested a ball, not a battle.

MANLY STYLE

The rapid expansion of the army increased its visibility, changing the popular perception of masculinity. This may well have assisted George – 'Beau' – Brummell's fashion revolution. A former cavalry officer, he insisted on simple but well-tailored garments, spotless white linen, highly polished boots and an erect bearing.

Regency 'exquisites' leaving their club in St James's. Wartime taxes on luxuries included a levy on wig-powder, which killed off the wearing of wigs. The top hat, introduced in 1797, became a sartorial sensation. The whips and boots imply a fashionable addiction to riding and hunting.

INTERNATIONAL IMPLICATIONS

French interruptions of Caribbean cane sugar imports encouraged British farmers to grow beet as an alternative, hastening the end of plantation slavery.

Britain's support for Spain's guerrilla war against French occupation led the grateful Spanish to send a whole flock of merino sheep to

George III, an avid agriculturalist. Within a decade the sheep were in Australia, transforming a money-draining penal colony into a booming asset.

French revolutionaries drove more than 2,000 Catholic clergy to exile in Britain. Thousands of Irish Catholics fought loyally in the British army. The English Catholic academy at St Omer relocated to Stonyhurst in Lancashire. These factors softened traditional bigotry towards the Roman Church, leading to the end of discrimination against Catholics in 1829.

Somebody else who fled France for the safety of England was Madame Tussaud, the Swiss drawing-teacher to the children of Marie Antoinette. With her she brought a grisly collection of wax death-masks.

Britain's grimmest prison, Dartmoor, was built to house French prisoners-of-war.

GETTING ORGANIZED

The need to organize the nation's resources efficiently for war led to:

- The development of the Ordnance Survey.

- The establishment of a Board of Agriculture and the first veterinary college.

- The building of London's enclosed docks.

- The first census.

- A huge expansion of the militia and volunteers.

- The construction of 103 defensive 'Martello Towers' to guard the coasts.

Meanwhile, fear of internal insurrection led to the proliferation of soup kitchens and the introduction of allotment gardens for vegetables. It also led to the spread of rural wage subsidies pioneered by the

THE PRICE OF VICTORY

Three things are needed for war – money, money and more money. England's wealth financed four coalitions of allies to fight Napoleon on land while she fought at sea. Financing the war led to the introduction of:

Income tax and money orders.

~

£5 notes, then £1 notes and notes printed with serial numbers.

The rebuilding of the Bank of England on a massive scale.

~

The rise of the Rothschild and Baring finance houses.

---

magistrates of Speenhamland, Berkshire. Later denounced as counter-productive interference with the price of labour, these subsidies may, nevertheless, have staved off mass rioting at the time.

LOVE OF COUNTRY

With Europe ravaged by war or under French occupation, English aristocrats' traditional 'Grand Tour' was suspended.

Heightened patriotism joined with necessity to create a new interest in British landscape, the emergence of 'Romanticism' and the exploration of 'picturesque' landscapes in the Lake District, Snowdonia and the Peaks.

So, writer and opium addict Thomas de Quincey set off to tour Wales with a tent – the first recorded camping holiday – while the new enthusiasm for the countryside was also reflected in the rise of the 'Norwich School' and the foundation of the English Water Colour Society. Wordsworth and Coleridge, meanwhile, found a receptive market for their *Lyrical Ballads*, which celebrated plain English speech and the beauties of Nature in England.

The enforced emphasis on domestic pleasures quickened interest in sport. Cricket witnessed the publication of the first coaching manual, the introduction of round-arm bowling, the opening of Lord's cricket ground and the inauguration of the Eton *versus* Harrow and Gentlemen *versus* Players matches. The 'Sport of Kings' was enriched by the laying out of Goodwood and the introduction of the Ascot Gold Cup and the 2,000 Guineas, while Britain's first boxing club was established by 'Gentleman' Jackson.

MARCH OF PROGRESS

The war led to various important changes. For example, the Army gradually adopted the rifle in place of the musket, as well as Major Shrapnel's explosive shell and Colonel Congreve's rockets. The Navy adopted Commander Beaufort's scale for measuring wind force and ordered its first supplies of canned food. At Portsmouth, Marc Brunel and Henry Maudslay championed integrated mass-production with machine tools, which enabled semi-skilled labourers to make pulley-blocks for ships' rigging.

The really momentous technological advances were largely unconnected with the military, however. These include: the world's first steam-powered ship, locomotive and printing-press; central heating; gas lighting; lithography; carbon paper; cotton sewing thread; and the miner's safety lamp.

Much else happened outside the backwash of war:

SIGHT FOR SORE EYES

British success in thwarting Napoleon's conquest of Egypt was achieved at the cost of most British troops contracting trachoma. The response was the establishment of Moorfields Eye Hospital as a specialist treatment unit.

- Jenner discovered vaccination.

- John Nash started building Regent Street.

- T. R. Malthus's *Essay on Population*, predicted that it would always outrun the world's food supply.

Regent Street offered up-market shopping for the affluent, but Nash's handsome colonnades became notorious for sheltering prostitutes and were demolished in the interests of morality. The street as it stands today is largely a rebuilding of the 1920s.

- William Blake wrote *Jerusalem*, the Taylor sisters wrote *Twinkle, Twinkle, Little Star* and Charles and Mary Lamb composed their *Tales from Shakespeare*.

- *The Observer*, *The Edinburgh Review* and the *Quarterly Review* all began publication.

- *Childe Harold* made Byron famous.

- England's first purpose-built picture gallery opened at Dulwich.

- Spencer Perceval became Britain's only Prime Minister to be assassinated.

In 1807 Parliament passed the first laws to regulate factory working hours and conditions. These proved entirely ineffectual. In same year Parliament also abolished the slave trade – definitively.

WOMEN AND CHILDREN FIRST!

In February 1852 HMS *Birkenhead*, an early iron-hulled vessel, was taking reinforcements to South Africa. Drawn from ten different regiments, with the largest contingent coming from the Black Watch, many were new recruits. Most of their women and children disembarked at Cape Town but 13 remained on board for the last leg of the journey.

On 25 February the ship struck an uncharted rock, smashing a massive hole in her hull. A hundred men drowned where they slept. Those who made it on deck rushed to man pumps and ready lifeboats only to find just two seaworthy. Within minutes the ship's back broke, sinking the front section. The surviving soldiers mustered in ranks on the rear section. Fearing a general rush might swamp the women and children's boat, Colonel Seton, the officer commanding, ordered the men to 'stand fast'. They did.

Six weeks later the *Illustrated London News* reported that, 'the coolness and steady obedience to order which the troops manifested on that awful and trying occasion present an instance of one of the noblest results of discipline.'

Most of the soldiers died – from drowning or sharks. Dozens swam ashore, two miles away; about 60, clinging to masts and rigging, were taken off by a rescue ship. As the muster rolls went down with the ship the number lost has never been exactly established. The original complement was about 640; fewer than 200 survived.

The event had an effect around the world. In London, Queen Victoria ordered a memorial for the Royal Hospital, Chelsea. King Frederick William of Prussia had an account of the men's bravery read out to every regiment in his army. A mountain and a river in British Columbia were named after the *Birkenhead*. And even 40 years after the incident, Thomas M. Hemy's painting *The Wreck of the Birkenhead* was widely popular as a print, reproduced in many schoolbooks.

✵ ALL CHANGE ON THE HOME FRONT ✵

Until August 1914 a sensible, law-abiding Englishman could pass through life and hardly notice the existence of the state, beyond the post office and the policeman.

A. J. P. TAYLOR, *ENGLISH HISTORY* 1914–1945

The First World War changed all that, leaving as permanent legacies state interventions such as compulsory passports, licensing hours, daylight saving time and government departments for science and industry. Anti-German feeling led the Royal Family to change its name from Saxe-Coburg-Gotha to Windsor, while new orders of chivalry – Companion of Honour and Order of the British Empire – were established for 'conspicuous national service.'

Financing the war led to the first flag days for charity, and the sale of National Savings certificates. More tangibly, working-class real incomes, allowing for inflation, rose by a fifth in four years.

Dealing with casualties led to the establishment of the first dedicated plastic surgery ward and the first psychiatric hospital. Military life also affected everyday civilian lifestyles, popularizing the trench coat, toothpaste (rather than tooth powder), 'safety' razors and zip-fasteners. And, to the benefit of children everywhere, the school-leaving age was raised to 14.

WOMEN GO TO WAR

Mother and I declared support of our country. She declared that the military situation imperatively required the admission of women to munitions factories... to liberate men for the front....

CHRISTABEL PANKHURST

Recruiting 5,000,000 men into the armed forces opened entirely new opportunities for women on an unprecedented scale. For the first time women became bus conductors, taxi drivers and bank cashiers. Emmeline Pankhurst and her daughter Christabel, who had built a superb propaganda organization to win the vote, turned to recruiting women for factories and men for the forces. The effects were dramatic:

- 100,000 women joined the armed forces
- 100,000 became nurses • 250,000 worked on farms
- 30,000 worked for the YMCA • 500,000 took on office jobs
- 1,600,000 went into industry • 400,000 left domestic service

In recognition of the critical role women had played in the war effort, in 1918 women were finally granted the right to vote – at the age of 30.

The impact of these changes was considerable. Factory working led women to adopt 'bobbed' hair and trousers. Stiff 'foundation garments' were replaced by the flexible brassiere. Women workers with their own earnings had new spending priorities. Unmarried girls began to wear make-up, smoke cigarettes in public and buy their own drinks

Votes for women, now! A Suffragette addresses an audience depicted as sceptical but genial. In reality suffragettes were often abused and sometimes attacked – on occasion with the connivance of police who refused to intervene.

in pubs. Married women bought false teeth and better food for their families. Marie Stopes's *Married Love* became the first generally available book to give frank information about birth control.

SECOND WORLD WAR

Lessons learned from the Home Front experience of the Great War proved of real benefit in the Second World War. Instead of hastily improvised food rationing, a scheme based on nutritional science was devised by Professor Jack Drummond of London University and was in position when war broke out. The ingenious 'points' system that ran parallel with money purchasing was the work of a schools inspector. Eventually 50,000 people were employed in the Ministry of Food administering the nation's diet. US administrators hailed it as the greatest success in public health policy in modern times.

The mobilization of labour was even more systematic. A system of 'reserved occupations' safeguarded highly skilled manpower for the war effort and protected such non-combatants from accusations of cowardice. Special talents were skilfully mobilized as stage-designers were put to work on camouflage and making decoy aerodromes, language experts set to interrogation and monitoring propaganda and mathematicians recruited for code-breaking. Radio comediennes Gert and Daisy encouraged housewives to try out economical recipes and radio gardening celebrity 'Mr Middleton' headed the 'Dig for Victory' campaign. Altogether a higher percentage of females was mobilized for war work in England than in totalitarian Nazi Germany.

Although civilian living standards overall fell 50 per cent during the war, the poorest were actually better off than they had been during the depression of the 1930s – and for the first time a glimpse of a brighter future was given in the form of chewing-gum, nylon stockings and penicillin.

5
YESTERDAY'S CELEBRITIES

Who knows whether…there be not more remarkable
persons forgot than any that stand remembered…?

SIR THOMAS BROWNE, 1658

This chapter is dedicated to the recognition that great fame has proved all too fugitive for countless heroes – and villains – whose names were once household words, memorialized by statues or street names.

✳ FLEETING FAME ✳

RESTORATION HUSTLER

Barbon Close, an uninviting cul-de-sac opposite Great Ormond Street Hospital for Children, commemorates the once notorious Dr Nicholas Barbon (?1640–98), London's first buccaneering property developer.

A qualified physician, Nicholas Barbon forsook medicine for the opportunities opened up by the Great Fire of 1666, which destroyed the heart of the ancient City and led to mass-migrations creating new suburbs from St James's to Spitalfields.

Barbon's opportunistic schemes had a 'no frills' approach, paring costs to a minimum and repeating standardized designs in squares and streets in the City, Soho and Holborn. His largest single venture was Red Lion Square, next to Gray's Inn, one of the four Inns of Court, where ambitious young men studied law seriously and fellow 'students' passed a couple of years play-going, gambling and drinking. When the lawyers in Gray's Inn realized they were going to lose their view they did not take Barbon to court but turned out with a hundred students to stop his workmen by force. Led by Barbon in person, the workmen won the day.

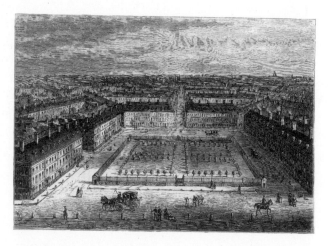

Barbon's biggest project – Red Lion Square, laid out on a seventeen-acre paddock in 1684. This engraving of 1725 shows that it was then only a few blocks from London's northern edge.

An inventive juggler with borrowed capital, Barbon was also an original economic thinker, one of the first to argue that value could be created by immaterial factors like changes in fashion, which made two coats of the same cloth different in price.

Barbon also founded London's first fire insurance company – the 'Insurance Office at the Backside of the Royal Exchange'. In 1698 he died as he had lived, massively in debt.

DARWIN'S INTELLECTUAL GRANDFATHER

John Ray (1627–1705) established 'species' as the fundamental category for classifying Nature.

In 1660 Ray published the first-ever comprehensive catalogue of the plants of an English locality, listing 626 varieties found around Cambridge. When his religious scruples killed his brilliant academic career, Ray roamed from the Netherlands to Malta, plant-hunting.

Isolated in his village birthplace, Black Notley in Essex, Ray single-handedly produced a comprehensive three volume *Historia Plantarum* (*History of Plants*, 1686–1704) and other works on birds, fishes and insects. Unlike previous naturalists Ray classified living things, not by size or colour or habitat, but by their *structure*, bringing a new precision to the systematic understanding of the natural world. In his own day, however, Ray was best known for *The Wisdom of God Manifested in the Works of Creation*, in which he deployed his vast learning to illustrate the design which underpinned all Nature. This work went through four editions before Ray's death and a fifteenth by 1827. The Ray Society, established in his honour in 1844, publishes books on British flora and fauna.

PRISONERS' FRIEND

Bedford magistrate and prison reformer John Howard (1726–90) was the first person to have a statue erected to his memory in St Paul's.

Howard's personal fortune allowed him to travel extensively until a run-in with a French privateer gave him a taste of imprisonment that shaped the rest of his life.

Appointed High Sheriff of Bedfordshire, Howard was shocked by the foul conditions in prisons, where gaolers lived by extorting 'fees' from inmates. Howard's crusade of four national and four European tours of inspection covered 50,000 miles to accumulate information that he placed before Parliament and public in a series of publications. This led to the abolition of gaolers' fees and improvements in prison health.

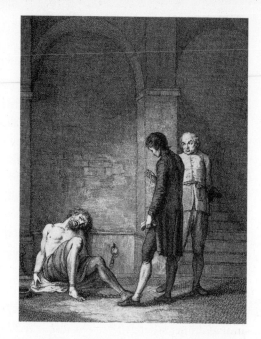

You should be so lucky! A visitor admonishes a lone, manacled prisoner under the eyes of a well-groomed gaoler. In reality most eighteenth-century prisons were foully overcrowded and run as family businesses by corrupt bullies.

Caring for a typhus victim on a journey to Russia, he died of the same disease. Recognized as a figure of European reputation, he was buried by the Russians with pomp and a marble memorial.

Devout, austere, teetotal and vegetarian, Howard spent £30,000 of his own money to fund the enquiries that finally cost him his life. In England his death was noted in the *London Gazette*, a unique distinction for a civilian. The memorial statue was paid for by public subscription, and the Howard League for Penal Reform is named in his honour.

LIFE SAVER

When any sick to me apply,
I physics, bleeds and sweats 'em.
If after that they choose to die,
Why verily – I Lettsom.

The pun is irresistible, but a slur all the same.

Born in the Virgin Islands, at his father's death Quaker physician John Coakley Lettsom (1744–1815) freed all his slaves, completely disinheriting himself. Trained at Edinburgh and Leyden, he amused his teachers with his eccentric practice of making careful case notes on individual patients. Lettsom began his career by opening the first free dispensary for the poor. Within 30 years, 40 more had opened throughout the country.

When only 29, Lettsom founded the Medical Society of London in a bid to end rivalries between physicians, surgeons and apothecaries by bringing together 30 of each for regular meetings of common professional concern. It is the oldest surviving medical society in England.

Lettsom was also a founding member of the Royal Humane Society to promote life-saving by artificial respiration and organized its annual dinner where the 'raised from the dead' processed round the table to applause. His last big project, the Royal Sea-Bathing Hospital at Margate, was the modern world's first open-air sanatorium.

By not taking a working day off in nineteen years, Lettsom earned a fabulous £12,000 a year. His villa, Grove Hill, Camberwell, had a splendid study suite of library, museum and hothouse and ten acres of grounds where he pioneered the cultivation of mangel-wurzels and sea kale. A guidebook of 1819 noted Camberwell's sole point of distinction as being the former residence of the 'late famous Dr Lettsom'.

TOWERING EGO

Mr Beckford has undoubtedly shown himself...
an accomplished patron of unproductive labour,
an enthusiastic collector of expensive trifles...

WILLIAM HAZLITT, 1824

High above Bath stands Beckford's Tower, a monument to the ego of a recluse. Novelist, painter, poseur, composer, connoisseur and compulsive collector, William Beckford (1759–1844) claimed to be descended from *all* the signatories of Magna Carta.

Inheriting a million pounds and an annual income of £100,000 – largely from slave plantations – Beckford got through most of it in a long life of self-indulgence. Forced abroad by a homosexual scandal, he was an eyewitness to the fall of the Bastille, accumulated a fabulous art collection and wrote an accomplished Oriental fantasy, *Vathek*, in French, in three days and two nights.

Beckford eventually spent £250,000 rebuilding the family seat of Fonthill in Wiltshire as a vast Gothic pile with an immense tower – which fell down, wrecking the house. Forced to sell off Fonthill and its contents, Beckford moved to Bath, where he bought three houses and began filling them up all over again. Beckford also bought a mile of land behind his houses to make a ride to the hill where his tower gave views over five counties.

Thwarted in having the tower as his mausoleum, Beckford was buried in its shadow. It is now a museum and education centre.

Left *Obtrusive for the reclusive. Beckford's Tower, overlooking Bath, was completed in 1827 to the designs of local architect, H. E. Goodridge.*

Opposite *The first Christmas card was designed in 1843 – at the suggestion of Henry Cole – by John Calcott Horsley R.A., brother-in-law of the engineer Isambard Kingdom Brunel. Because the card shows a family drinking a toast it was denounced for encouraging drunkenness. Christmas cards did not become generally popular until the 1860s.*

RENAISSANCE MAN – VICTORIAN STYLE

The Henry Cole Wing of the Victoria & Albert Museum is named after its first Director.

Prince Albert supplied the vision for the Great Exhibition of 1851. Sir Henry Cole (1808–82) made it happen. Afterwards he acquired many exhibits as the core collection of what was originally 'The Museum of Manufactures'.

A talented watercolourist, Cole also learned to engrave and etch well enough to exhibit at the Royal Academy. He also won a prize for designing a postage stamp and another for a tea service mass-produced by Minton.

Thanks to Cole, Britain gained a purpose-built Public Record Office, its first government Department of Art and Science, a national network of art schools, the Royal Albert Hall, the Royal College of Music and a National School of Cookery.

A self-appointed high priest of public improvement, Cole also interested himself in electric lighting, tree-planting and the productive use of sewage. In retirement he edited the *Complete Works* of satirical novelist and poet Thomas Love Peacock and worked on a scheme to have convicts make street signs and house numbers out of mosaic. Henry Cole also invented the Christmas card – but never bothered to patent the idea.

SUPER SWINDLER

Born Albert Gottheimer, Baron Grant (1830–99) was the most un-scrupulous company promoter of the nineteenth century, losing at least £20,000,000 belonging to the 'small yet sanguine investors' who trusted him with their cash.

Some of Grant's schemes *did* work out (hence the Italian barony for funding Milan's famous shopping-arcade) but most of the mines, railways, waterworks and banks for which he took the savings of vicars, widows and orphans were either ill-founded or outright fraudulent.

Grant made a bid for public respectability by paying for the gardens of London's Leicester Square and buying Sir Edwin Landseer's portrait of Sir Walter Scott for the National Portrait Gallery.

Meanwhile he lavished money on building Kensington House as the largest private residence in London, with a hundred rooms and grounds with an Italian garden, an orangery, aviary, bowling-alley, skating-rink and three-acre lake.

In 1875, when Grant was at the peak of success, Anthony Trollope published *The Way We Live Now*, whose villainous 'hero', Augustus Melmotte, was a very thinly disguised portrait of the arch-fraudster.

Besieged by 89 separate lawsuits, Grant was forced to sell his art collection. Kensington House was used just once, for a 'Bachelors' Ball', then seized by his creditors, sold off for a paltry £10,461 and demolished. Grant retired to the south coast fending off enraged victims to the last.

Opposite *Superbly illustrated and with a text in both English and French, Domenico Angelo's L'école des Armes was first published in 1763 and reprinted in 1765 and again in 1767. Angelo's pupils included the controversial radical John Wilkes and the dramatist Sheridan. The Carlisle House academy brought Angelo a handsome income of £4,000 a year.*

✳ SPORTING SUPERSTARS ✳

FATHER OF FENCING

Although duelling was illegal in England by the eighteenth century, swordsmanship was still part of a gentleman's education.

Born in Italy and trained in Paris, Domenico Angelo (Malevolti Tremamondo, 1716–1802) became riding and fencing instructor to the future George III. In an encounter that made him famous, Angelo was matched against Keynes, an Irish master. Angelo warded off every attack with ease, landed half a dozen perfect hits and ending by disarming his opponent.

Angelo then opened London's most prestigious school of arms at Carlisle House, Soho, and published the definitive illustrated treatise on fencing. He sent his son, Henry, to Eton, then retired there himself, giving fencing lessons virtually until his death aged 86.

Henry moved the academy to fashionable Bond Street, taught Byron and the Prince Regent to fence, and then retired to write entertainingly unreliable memoirs. The Angelo academy continued in family ownership until 1866.

CHAMPION OF THE WORLD

Daniel Mendoza (?1765–1836) was only 5 feet 6 inches tall and never weighed more than 160 pounds, but from 1792 until 1795 he was boxing champion of all England – which meant, in effect, of the world.

Born in Aldgate, 'Mendoza the Jew' learned to fight simply to defend himself and his employer from gratuitous insults.

Before the adoption of the 'Queensberry rules', bare-knuckle boxers fought to exhaustion or a knockout, with contests often lasting an hour or more. In his first major fight, at Barnet racecourse in April 1787, Mendoza beat Samuel Martin, 'the Bath Butcher', in just twenty minutes.

Richard Humphries (left), initially the teacher of Mendoza (right), fought him three times. The first contest ended when Mendoza sprained a foot but Mendoza won both the other fights.

Mendoza's compact physique would never have enabled him to become Britain's first sporting superstar without a superior style to outclass far larger opponents. Relying on speedy footwork and the entirely new idea of landing punches in swift combinations, Mendoza disorientated bewildered opponents, darting away from retaliation. Placing the utmost emphasis on balance, Mendoza set out his methods in *The Art of Boxing*, the first work to treat the sport 'scientifically'.

Mendoza was finally defeated by 'Gentleman' Jackson, with the very un-gentlemanly tactic of grabbing Mendoza's long hair and pummelling him in the face.

In 1806, although over 40, Mendoza still won a contest of 53 rounds. Semi-retired, he then made profitable sparring tours, ran a pub, played fives and had 11 children.

PEERLESS PEDESTRIAN

Robert Barclay Allardice (1779–1854) once got up at five o'clock in the morning, walked 30 miles shooting game, walked 60 miles home to change, then 16 miles to a ball, walked back by seven o'clock the following morning and spent the next day shooting.

Strikingly handsome and able to lift half a ton, 'Captain Barclay' was a soldier by profession and a 'pedestrian' of national renown. In 1801 he walked 110 miles round a muddy park in 19 hours 27 minutes. In 1802 he covered 64 miles in just 10 hours and in 1805 walked 72 miles between breakfast and dinner.

Barclay's most famous feat was performed at Newmarket in 1809 when he walked a full mile in each of 1,000 successive hours, losing 32 pounds in weight. Five days later he went off with the abortive expedition to seize the Dutch island of Walcheren. Barclay lived to be 75 when he died after being kicked by a horse.

'SQUIRE OF ENGLAND'

Excelling at every country sport, George Osbaldestone (1787–1866) had the best pack of foxhounds in the country and also played cricket for the MCC, once achieving the bowler's supreme triumph of taking all ten wickets in an innings. On another occasion he helped to win a match at Lord's while playing with a fractured shoulder.

This was entirely in character. A fine shot, superb horseman and outstanding athlete, Osbaldestone once beat the real tennis champions of France and Italy using only his gloved hand against their rackets.

In 1831, at the age of 44, Osbaldestone wagered 1,000 guineas he could ride 200 miles in 10 hours. Changing mounts every four miles, he managed to average 26 miles an hour and beat the deadline with 78 minutes to spare.

At 66, Osbaldestone went 72 hours without sleep in a marathon billiards match and at just short of 80, confined to a bath-chair by gout, he won a bet by sitting for an entire day without moving once.

'THE LITTLE WONDER'

In 1850 diminutive John Wisden (1826–84), playing for 'The North', clean bowled the entire batting order of 'The South', a cricketing feat never achieved before or since. Wisden also organized the first English cricket tour of North America, in one match taking six wickets in successive balls, another unique record.

After coaching at Harrow, Wisden took over a Sussex pub – inevitably named The Cricketers – and opened a West End shop selling cricket gear and cigars. In 1864 he published the first edition of *Wisden's Cricketer's Almanac*. This became the *nonpareil* of sporting publications, despite the fact that the initial volume also included the rules of quoits, interesting facts about canals and coinage and a concise history of China.

THE MAN WHO INVENTED THE CUP

'The forgotten father of modern sport', according to the Football Association's own official historian, was Charles Alcock (1842–1907). Educated at Harrow, Alcock founded the famous Wanderers football team that won the FA Cup five times between 1872 and 1878. As secretary of the FA, Alcock started its cup competition, based on an inter-house knock-out event at Harrow. In 1875 Alcock captained England against Scotland and two weeks later refereed the Cup Final. Ten years later he persuaded the FA to accept professionalism, heading off a split that would divide rugby a decade later.

Alcock played cricket for the Gentlemen of Essex, was secretary of Surrey County Cricket Club, vice-President of the Royal Mid-Surrey Golf Club, chairman of the Richmond Athletic Association, a prolific contributor to *The Field* and *The Sportsman*, and a pioneering historian of sport.

ILL-FATED FRED

The son of a winner of the Grand National, Fred Archer (1857–86) became champion jockey at 16 and remained so for 13 successive seasons, winning 21 classic races and riding 2,748 winners.

Severely depressed by the death of his first child and then of his wife, Archer ruined his health with a training diet of toast, castor oil and tea laced with gin. On the second anniversary of his wife's death Archer shot himself, leaving a fortune of £66,000 and a nation in mourning.

WIMBLEDON WONDER

At the age of 15 Charlotte 'Lottie' Dod (1871–1960) became the youngest ever winner of the Wimbledon women's singles title. She went on to win it another four times, as well as holding ten other tournament titles, before retiring from tennis at the age of 21.

In 1899 and 1900 Dod played hockey for England and in 1904 won the British Ladies Open Golf Championship. In 1908 she won a silver medal in the women's archery event at the London Olympic Games.

Dressed for success. The informal dress worn by the barely teenage Lottie Dod may have given her a significant edge on court over older opponents more cumbrously dressed and coiffeured.

An expert skater, Lottie Dod was also proficient at rowing, riding, mountaineering and billiards. An accomplished pianist and enthusiastic singer of madrigals, she was awarded the Red Cross Gold Medal for outstanding service as a nurse during the First World War. She devoted her adult life to running a girls' club in Whitechapel.

BODY BEAUTIFUL

Born Friedrich Wilhelm Muller in Konigsberg, East Prussia, Eugen Sandow (1867–1925) ran away to dodge military service and took up weightlifting, developing an expanded chest size of 62 inches.

Circus acrobat, wrestler and music hall 'strongman', Sandow became a naturalized Briton and in 1891 organized the first-ever international weightlifting competition. In 1897 he opened an 'institute of physical culture' in the former Angelo school of arms.

Sandow's empire expanded with the publication of a manual – *Strength and How to Obtain It* – a monthly magazine, *Physical Culture*,

Riding to riches. Even when working as a music hall strongman Sandow could earn £150 a week, equal to the average annual wage of the men who made up most of his audiences.

a correspondence course, the opening of six more centres and a mail-order business for health-related products, ranging from cocoa to corsets.

In 1908 Sandow's £1,500 gift made him the largest individual donor to the appeal for London's Olympic stadium. He then offered free physical training to the newly formed Territorial Army and was appointed 'professor of physical culture to the king'.

By the time the First World War broke out Sandow was so popular he entirely escaped the Germanophobia which smeared even members of the royal family.

Eugen Sandow died in 1925, not yet 60. There was no post-mortem but the recorded cause of his demise was consistent with syphilis. His wife had him buried in an unmarked grave and within a month she and his daughters had disappeared abroad.

GREEK GOD

*This young man attracted universal admiration by
his uncommon beauty. He was of impressive stature,
tall, well-proportioned, his hair and complexion
of surprising fairness.*

OLYMPIC GAMES OFFICIAL REPORT

In the first modern Olympics, held in Athens in 1896, Eugen Sandow's protégé, Launceston Elliot (1874–1930), became the only Briton ever to win a gold medal at weightlifting.

Handsome as a Greek god, Elliot delighted his Greek hosts by winning the One-Handed Lift, coming second in the Two-Handed Lift, fourth in the heavyweight division of Greco-Roman wrestling and running in the hundred metres. Elliot later togged himself up as a Roman gladiator to go on the music hall stage and eventually retired to Australia.

THE MIRACLE-WORKER

'Sam' Mussabini (1867–1927) was not himself a sporting superstar – he made them. In the Oscar-winning film *Chariots of Fire* Mussabini is portrayed as the gruff, passionate taskmaster who drove highly strung Harold Abrahams towards a sprinter's gold at the 1924 Paris Olympics.

Presented to the audience as part-Italian, part-Arab, Mussabini was in fact a born Londoner – of Syrian-Italian-French descent. A sprinter and sporting journalist, Mussabini coached Bert Harris to win Britain's first professional cycling championship, founded a monthly magazine (*World of Billiards*) and in three weeks coached South African Reggie Walker to take gold in the 100 metres at the 1908 London Olympics.

Over the course of five Olympics between 1908 and 1928 six of Mussabini's protégés garnered eleven medals between them. In 1923–24 he helped Vera Palmer-Searle set three women's world sprint records.

Appointed Britain's first professional athletics coach in 1912, Sam Mussabini lived in a house backing onto Herne Hill Stadium until his death from diabetes aged 60. The Mussabini Medal for outstanding achievement by a British coach was established by the National Coaches' Foundation in 1998.

THE ULTIMATE ALL-ROUNDER

The sporting career of Charles Burgess – 'C. B.' – Fry (1872–1956) ran from the age of W. G. Grace to the advent of television.

Fry played football for the Casuals before he left Repton and cricket for Surrey before going to Oxford – where he won 'Blues' for football, cricket and athletics and set a new *world* record for the long jump.

As a professional cricketer with Sussex and Hampshire, Fry played in 26 Test matches for England. In 1901 he finished top of the batting averages for the first of six times and became the first player ever to hit centuries in six successive innings.

Fry also played football regularly for the Corinthians and appeared for Southampton in the 1902 Cup Final. He went on to invent the idea of interviewing other sportsmen – and was allegedly also offered the throne of Albania.

✺ FORGOTTEN FEMALES ✺

History, real solemn history, I cannot be interested in…
the men all so good for nothing and hardly any women at all.

JANE AUSTEN, *NORTHANGER ABBEY*, 1818

LIVING BY HER WITS

Aphra Behn (1640–89), christened Ayfara Johnson, was the first woman in England to earn a living as a professional writer.

As a child Aphra lived in Surinam, the future Dutch Guiana but then English, where she saw slavery at first hand. Briefly married, she was left destitute by the sudden death of her husband (a London merchant of Dutch descent) and was recruited to spy in Antwerp for the English government under the code name Astraea – later her literary *nom de plume*.

Fending off numerous assaults on her virtue gave Aphra Behn experience that she later turned to advantage for the stage, but also enabled her to learn the Dutch were planning a surprise raid on the English navy. Surviving shipwreck on the way home, Aphra passed on her warning but was ignored. The Dutch duly burned the English fleet at anchor in the Medway. Behn was never paid for her efforts, forcing her temporarily into debtor's prison.

Aphra Behn's novel, *Oronooko* (1688), an account of a slave revolt in Suriname led by a noble African prince, was the earliest English work to expose the horrors of slavery, and to give a sympathetic depiction of the non-European characters.

CUTTING EDGE

At 74, twice-widowed Mary Granville Delany (1700–88) invented a new art form to amuse the royal family. She called her creations 'paper mosaics'. They would now be known as découpage or collage.

Made of precisely cut, intricate layers of coloured paper, they represented botanical specimens with astonishing accuracy and were praised by Sir Joseph Banks, the President of the Royal Society, as 'the only imitations of nature I have seen from which I would venture to describe botanically any plant without the least fear of committing an error.'

Mrs Delany completed almost 980 specimens until, in 1784, her eyesight failed.

Six volumes of posthumous autobiography and letters revealed a well-connected, well-read, waspish woman who came into her own when most of her contemporaries were in their dotage or dead. The *Flora Delanica* are now in the British Library.

BARONESS BOUNTIFUL

The youngest of six siblings, Angela Burdett-Coutts (1814–1906) was carefully selected to become sole heiress to the fortune of her banker grandfather Thomas Coutts, and would give away some £4,000,000.

Her causes included night shelters for the homeless, housing, education, victims of famine and war, the rehabilitation of prostitutes and sponsored emigration. Her many enthusiasms ranged from the protection of donkeys to the creation of youth clubs, public fountains and sewing schools. She sponsored the foundation of Anglican bishoprics in Adelaide, Cape Town and British Columbia, and founded a factory making artificial flowers to employ disabled girls.

Opposite *Initially married to a drunken gambler, Mrs Delany found happiness with an elderly Irish clergyman. Her friends included Jonathan Swift, Edmund Burke, John Wesley and Horace Walpole.*

Right *Suitably gushing. An elaborate fountain in Victoria Park in London's East End, the first park purposely laid out for the benefit of the poor, is the main memorial to the generosity of Angela Burdett-Coutts.*

Sometimes she made mistakes. Columbia Market, a massive Gothic trading hall costing £200,000 was shunned until finally demolished half a century after her death.

In 1871 Angela Burdett-Coutts was created a baroness in her own right, the first woman so honoured for public service. At 67 she appalled Queen Victoria by marrying an American almost 40 years younger than herself – and lived on for another 25 years.

THE GREAT CRUSADER

Married to a university teacher, Josephine Butler (1828–1906) was initially involved in the campaign to open higher education to women. At the age of 35, however, her life was shattered by the death of her only daughter, aged five, in a fall before her very eyes.

Butler, living in Liverpool, threw herself into founding night shelters for women and rehabilitating prostitutes. At that very time

'Contagious Diseases Acts' were passed in 1864, 1866 and 1869 to limit the spread of sexually transmitted infections in seaports and garrison towns. These laws empowered police to detain any woman even *suspected* of being a prostitute and force them to undergo a humiliating medical examination.

The blatantly discriminatory nature of these laws, throwing the entire blame for infection on a single sex, provoked the formation of a Ladies National Association for Repeal. As Honorary Secretary, Josephine Butler devoted her life to the 'Great Crusade' until repeal was finally achieved in 1886.

Butler continued to campaign across Europe against licensed brothels, 'white slavery' and child prostitution, profoundly influencing the state regulation of 'vice' in France, Italy, Switzerland, Norway and the Netherlands.

SLUM SAVIOUR

Remembered as a founder of the National Trust, Octavia Hill (1838–1912) was also the godmother of a novel profession – housing manager.

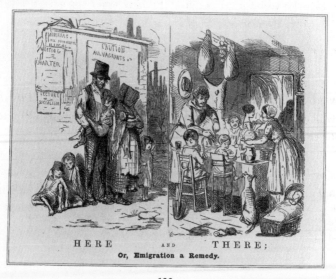

HERE AND THERE;
Or, Emigration a Remedy.

In 1864 Octavia Hill took over a decrepit row of artisan cottages in Marylebone. The progressive formula of the day was to replace slums with 'model dwellings' on the same site. Invariably built to a lower density per acre, these diminished the available housing stock, forcing the displaced to add to overcrowding elsewhere. Octavia Hill's much more economical and less disruptive solution was a thoroughgoing refurbishment.

Her other major innovation was managerial – collecting rents weekly in person. This enabled her to weed out feckless tenants and encourage the satisfactory. Once her financial backers' 5 per cent return had been achieved, any surplus was spent on projects like playgrounds or activities like sewing circles.

Octavia Hill's 'small is beautiful' approach eventually led to her managing 6,000 properties, attracting to her service:

- Henrietta Barnett, creator of Toynbee Hall (the first 'university settlement') and the prime mover behind Hampstead Garden Suburb.

- Beatrice Webb, co-founder of the *New Statesman* and the London School of Economics.

- Emma Cons, creator of the 'Old Vic' theatre and Morley College for adult education.

Octavia herself became co-founder of the Charity Organisation Society, which brought a new professionalism to well-meaning but often chaotic charities.

Opposite *Ticket to Paradise. Many philanthropists agreed that the best hope for Britain's destitute was a one-way ticket to the empty lands of an ever-expanding empire. Emigration peaked in the years 1911-13, when 1 per cent of the entire population of the British Isles was emigrating each year, with Canada as the most favoured destination.*

P. E. PIONEER

Martina Bergman-Osterberg (1849–1915) invented the games mistress and the gymslip.

A governess and librarian, Martina was 30 before entering Sweden's Royal Central Gymnastics Institute, where she learned the scientific physical education system developed by Per Hendrik Ling on the basis of human physiology.

In 1881 Bergman-Osterberg was hired by the new London School Board to train its elementary school teachers. Although convinced of the Ling system, Bergman-Osterberg privately believed London's children, damaged by inadequate diet and bad housing, would gain little from physical education alone. In 1885, therefore, she founded Britain's first physical education college to produce teachers for girls' private secondary schools by training them in anatomy, physiology, gymnastics and team games.

The appalling state of Britain's youth revealed by medical inspections of volunteers for the Boer War in South Africa led to a campaign for 'national efficiency'. By 1905 there were five more training colleges, two of them founded by Bergman-Osterberg's own former students. The Ling system then spread to boys' public schools and the Royal Navy and ultimately created another new profession – physiotherapy.

WORDS AND DEEDS

Mary Arnold (1851–1920) grew up in a Victorian Oxford consumed with religious controversy. As Mrs Humphry Ward she moved to London and from this detached perspective wrote the novel that made her notorious. *Robert Elsmere* tells the story of an idealistic clergyman who rejects Oxford's squabbling over incense and altar rails in order to tackle the urgent social horrors and spiritual void of the slums.

Former Prime Minister Gladstone reviewed the book as an attack on Christianity itself. It nevertheless sold 70,000 copies. The success of a pirated American edition secured Mrs Ward a US advance of £7,000 for her next effort, enabling her to buy a country house and take long holidays in Italy.

Mrs Ward did not, however, leave doing good to her fiction. In 1890 she established a university settlement notable for providing play facilities for children. She also pioneered the novel idea that children with disabilities should not simply be discarded, but rather should be provided with appropriate support in learning.

Mrs Ward's decision to head the Women's National Anti-Suffrage League cost her popularity but the Allied propaganda she wrote during the First World War recouped it, gaining her a CBE, an honorary degree from Edinburgh and the invitation to become one of England's first seven female magistrates. Unfortunately by then her health, never robust, had been totally undermined by her exertions, while her finances had been undermined by her husband's massive gambling debts.

The Mary Ward Centre survives to this day, though her role as a pioneer of 'special needs' education has been largely forgotten.

FOR VALOUR

BROTHERS IN ARMS

Noel Chavasse (1884–1917) was the only combatant in the First World War to be awarded the Victoria Cross twice.

Born in Oxford, twins Noel and Christopher Chavasse grew up in Liverpool, where their father was Anglican bishop. Both ran for Britain at the 1908 Olympics. Both entered Trinity College, Oxford.

Noel trained as a surgeon, joining the Royal Army Medical Corps. Christopher followed his father into the church. When war broke out Christopher was first overseas, as an army chaplain. Noel became medical officer of the Tenth Battalion (Liverpool Scottish) of the King's (Liverpool) Regiment.

Having already won the Military Cross, Noel Chavasse was award-ed the Victoria Cross for carrying 20 casualties to safety under fire in July 1916. A year later Noel Chavasse, despite multiple wounds, tended the wounded for two days under fire until he was killed by an artillery shell, which destroyed his aid post. For this action he was awarded a posthumous bar to his VC.

Christopher Chavasse was awarded the Military Cross, the Croix de Guerre and the Order of the British Empire (Military Division) for acts of gallantry in the field. He returned to Oxford to become the first Master of St Peter's College on New Inn Hall Street, where he and his brother had been born. He died in 1962.

GOLDEN BOY

On 4 July 1941, American Independence Day, Secretary for Air Sir Archibald Sinclair unveiled a plaque in the crypt of St Paul's Cathedral bearing the name of William Meade Lindley Fiske III and the inscrip-tion: 'An American Citizen Who Died That England Might Live'. The 'wings' from Fiske's pilot's uniform are still beneath it.

Born to a wealthy banking family, at the age of 16 'Billy' Fiske (1912–41) led the US bobsled team to gold at the first ever Winter Olympics.

A keen golfer and speed addict, the handsome playboy banker also co-produced a movie and married the Countess of Warwick. In 1939 Fiske joined the RAF using faked Canadian papers and was posted to 601 'Millionaire's Squadron' at Tangmere, Sussex. Fiske proved a nat-ural pilot, although he was never formally credited with a kill.

After just a month Fiske took a bullet in his petrol tank but, despite burns to hands and ankles, managed to nurse his plane back, gliding in with a stalled engine as Tangmere itself was under attack. The Hurricane burst into flames on landing but Billy was dragged out only to die the following day, aged 29 – one of nine American pilots to be numbered among 'the Few'.

6

THE INNER MAN – AND WOMAN

England has forty-two religions but only two sauces.

VOLTAIRE, *LETTERS ON ENGLAND*, 1733

Throughout history the largest part of human effort has been spent on producing, transporting, selling, preparing, consuming and appreciating food and drink. The nourishment of the nation is an inevitable part of every people's story.

THE LAST FAMINE

The Irish famine of the 1840s may well have cost one million lives – a population disaster unparalleled in the modern history of Europe. England, by contrast, had its last real famine in the 1620s.

Famine kills more by sickness than starvation, since it forces people to harvest hedgerows, in the process ingesting toxic roots and herbs to combat hunger. Weakened bodies, especially those of the very young and old, are vulnerable to dysentery or infectious diseases, and these diseases are then transported by survivors fleeing to other towns.

Medieval England's population expanded until the most productive lands were at full stretch, and runs of bad harvests in 1293–95 and 1310–12 soon led to famines. Between 1315 and 1318 catastrophic weather and a livestock epidemic caused a general European food crisis, which in England killed perhaps one in six.

When the Black Death removed a further third of the population in 1348–49 and 1361 it drastically reduced the pressure on land. Even so, wet summers and bad harvests caused famines in 1371, 1383 and 1437–39.

By the mid-sixteenth century population pressure was again reaching critical levels. Bad harvests in 1555–57, coinciding with an influenza epidemic, carried off some 200,000 people – more than 5 per cent of the population. Poor harvests and plague brought another crisis in 1594–98. Even in wealthy London, which imported food from abroad, martial law was declared.

There were regional disasters after that, in parts of Devon and Staffordshire, but England's last general famine years, 1622–4, spared the south and Midlands, hitting hardest in remote, upland areas such as Cumbria.

Efforts against famine gradually paid dividends. Emergency procedures, ordered by Cardinal Wolsey as far back as 1527, empowered magistrates to make compulsory purchases of hoarded grain and distribute it at need. Later on, England benefited from progressive increases in food supply thanks to:

- The draining of the Fens.

- The adoption of advanced farming techniques from the Low Countries.

- The increasing interest landlords took in improving their estates.

- More and better roads, improved river navigations and a larger coastal shipping fleet, allowing supplies to be sent to areas of shortage.

✸ FAST FOODS AND FISHY TALES ✸

On Palm Sunday, 1466, a party of Bohemian churchmen visiting Salisbury was entertained to 'an unbelievably costly banquet lasting three hours' that included a most puzzling course:

> *…it was roasted and looked like a duck. It has its*
> *wings, feathers, neck and feet. It lays eggs and tastes*
> *like a wild duck…in my mouth it turned to*
> *meat…they say…it grows first out of a worm in*
> *the sea…. It seeks its nourishment in the sea….*
> *Therefore it is said to be a fish.*

The curious course was, in fact, a barnacle goose. Technically classified as a fish by ingenious medieval churchmen, it was permitted for days of fasting when meat was otherwise forbidden. Another dodge was treating exotic items as medicines or aids to digestion – which made it all right to eat imported currants, dates and figs.

By the thirteenth century the entire Catholic world was supposed to keep 200 fast days a year, when meat, milk and eggs were prohibited and only fish and vegetables allowed:

- For the six weeks of Lent the pious were supposed to take only one meal a day.

- The fasting staple was salted herring, which the English made palatable with fiery mustard.

- The peasants' usual filler, a thick 'pottage' of peas flavoured with bacon, was replaced with dried peas boiled in water and flavoured with onions.

- The wealthy, not allowed milk, could replace it with a 'milk' made of ground almonds. In 1286 the household of King Edward I got through 28,500 pounds of almonds.

Frontispiece of the fourth (1652) edition of The Secrets of Angling *by John Dennys. The author, from Pucklechurch in Gloucestershire, died in 1609 and a first edition appeared posthumously in 1613. The figure on the left proclaims 'Well fayre the pleasure that brings such treasure', the one on the right 'Hold hooke and line, then all is mine.'*

In England 'fish days' continued for a century after the country broke away from the Catholic Church.

Elizabeth I banned meat in favour of fish not only on Fridays but Wednesdays and Saturdays as well. The rationale was pure patriotism – a big fishing fleet in time of peace meant a strong navy in time of war.

THE PENNY UNIVERSITIES

...these houses, which are very numerous in London, are extremely convenient. You have all manner of news there; you have a good fire, which you may sit by as long as you please; you have a dish of coffee; you meet your friends for the transaction of business, and all for a penny, if you don't care to spend more.

HENRI MISSON DE VALBURG, 1698

What sort of place combined the provision of liquid refreshment and snacks with the functions of shipping office, poste restante, chess club, lecture theatre, auction room, newspaper archive, debating society, travel bureau, gambling den, lending library, ticket agency, lost property office, Masonic lodge, adult education institute, employment exchange and consulting room? The answer is an eighteenth-century coffee house.

England's first coffee house was opened in Oxford in 1650 by Jacob the Jew. As the country was then under Puritan rule, which disapproved of taverns, the prospects for a new venue for socializing were good. Brewers and vintners sensed a threat and used the courts and the pamphlet press to attack coffee houses as fire hazards, sources of 'evil smells', centres of political intrigue and purveyors of an alien brew that caused impotence. Their opposition slackened when coffee houses began to sell upmarket wines and strong ales as well as coffee and chocolate.

In the West End of London, in the fashionable spa city of Bath and in the university cities of Oxford and Cambridge, coffee houses served as social clubs for wits, critics poets and scholars – hence their title of 'penny universities'.

Around Westminster coffee houses took on a political hue, serving as arenas of debate and informal headquarters for factions and cliques. In 1675, condemning coffee houses as 'the great resort of idle and disaffected persons', Charles II tried to close them down. Such was the outcry, the ban lasted just ten days.

CAFÉ CULTURE

Coffee houses were also invaluable to travellers and single men, especially men on the make. Lodging in single rooms, usually without cooking facilities, such men were unable either to feed themselves satisfactorily or to entertain others impressively. The coffee house enabled them to do both.

It therefore became customary for members of the floating male population of a big city to let it be known that they could be found daily at a particular coffee house between particular hours – letters and messages sent there would be sure to find them.

Foreign visitors were struck by the range of social types to be found in a coffee house and took this as evidence of the unusual egalitarianism of English society. But in the court suburb of St James the elite clientele of their coffee houses favoured their transformation into exclusive gentlemen's clubs, often devoted to high stakes gambling. The well-known club White's, for example, began as a 'chocolate house' run by Italian Francesco Bianco – who obligingly Anglicized his name to become Francis White.

WHEELING AND DEALING

Coffee houses in the City of London and bustling ports like Bristol and Newcastle were primarily places of business:

Lloyd's insurance market evolved from the coffee house kept by Edward Lloyd.

The Stock Exchange grew out of Jonathan's coffee house, while the Baltic Exchange, which handles shipping services, grew out of the Maryland.

Garraway's served as an auction house for two centuries.

As names like the Jamaica, the New York and the Pennsylvania suggest, many specialized in dealings with a particular place.

Doctors used coffee houses as consulting rooms.

Publishers and litigants in need of a hack writer or lawyer could be sure of finding one in the coffee houses around Fleet Street.

Coffee houses continued to flourish into the early nineteenth century when dramatic reductions in the taxes charged on coffee meant that it was no longer an expensive – and therefore exclusive – drink. This was the death-knell of the coffee house as a social institution and the beginning of its decline into a mere coffee *shop*.

✷ PLAIN COOKING ✷

...if Gentlemen will have French Cooks, they must pay for French Tricks. A Frenchman, in his own Country, would dress a fine Dinner of twenty Dishes...for the Expense he will put an English Lord to for dressing one dish...

HANNAH GLASSE, *THE ART OF COOKERY MADE PLAIN AND EASY*, 1747

Until the mid-eighteenth century, cookery books in England were written by men and dominated by French ideas of what good food was and how it should be prepared.

Hannah Glasse (1708–70) set out to break the mould. Her name became famous but the details of her life remain obscure. Neither the date of her birth, nor that of her death, are certain. She claimed to be dressmaker to the Princess of Wales and may have been married to a lawyer. Whatever her background, she had a mission:

> I have attempted…[what]…Nobody has yet thought worth their while…. If I have not wrote in the high polite Stile I hope I shall be forgiven, for my Intention is to instruct the lower Sort and therefore must treat them in their own way…when I bid them lard a Fowl, if I should bid them lard with large Lardoons, they would not know what I meant. But when I say…little Pieces of Bacon they know….

Hannah Glasse's purpose was not so much to make cooking plain and easy, but to make the *explanation* of it so, promising that 'every Servant who can but read will be capable of making a tolerable good Cook and those who have the least Notion of Cooking can't miss of being very good ones.'

Glasse's husband died in 1747, the year in which The Art of Cookery *was first published. Despite its success in going straight into a second edition, she was obliged to go into the clothing business with her daughter and went bankrupt. Forced to sell her precious copyright, she wrote further works but none enjoyed the same succes as* The Art of Cookery *and she died in poverty and obscurity.*

The Art of Cookery Made Plain and Easy, which Far Exceeds any Thing of the Kind ever yet Published…By a Lady, London was first published by the author in 1747 and by 1765 had been through nine, considerably enlarged, editions. An American edition appeared as late as 1805.

Mrs Glasse was not above lifting about a quarter of her recipes from other writers without acknowledgment but didn't miss the chance to drag in the name of the royal physician, Dr Richard Meade, as the source of her 'Certain Cure for the Bite of a Mad Dog'. On the other hand she did give the first known recipe for gooseberry fool.

✳ A PURE PINTA? ✳

A century before the medical profession learned how germs cause infection the novelist Tobias Smollett (1721–77), himself a trained doctor, showed a lively grasp of the notion in his description of the milk sold on the streets:

> …the produce of faded cabbage-leaves and sour draff [brewer's waste], lowered with hot water, frothed with bruised snails, carried through the streets in open pails, exposed to foul rinsings discharged from doors and windows, spittle, snot and tobacco-quids from foot-passengers, overflowings from mudcarts, spatterings from coach-wheels, dirt and trash chucked into it by roguish boys for the joke's sake, the spewings of infants, who have slobbered in the tin-measure…and finally the vermin that drops from the rags of the nasty drab that vends this precious mixture…

TOBIAS SMOLLETT, *THE EXPEDITION OF HUMPHREY CLINKER*, 1771

Even in the nineteenth century milk was still routinely adulterated with 10 to 50 per cent water. The coming of railways, however, not only made it possible to bring fresh supplies from the countryside but eventually killed off the business of keeping stall-fed cows in the backstreets of Britain's big cities. Meanwhile, co-operative societies, leaders in ethical retailing, made great play of running their own farms and dairies.

In 1860 French scientist Louis Pasteur discovered how to sterilize milk by heating it but hostile myths about the process, especially in Britain, delayed its general introduction on a commercial basis for another half century.

THE ENEMY WITHIN

Tobias Smollett not only knew how milk could be fouled but also how foods were made from foul ingredients, describing London bread as, 'a deleterious paste, mixed up with chalk, alum and bone-ashes.' The beer was, 'guiltless of hops and malt, vapid and nauseous; much fitter to facilitate the operation of a vomit, than to quench thirst and promote digestion'; and the butter a 'tallowy rancid mass...manufactured with candle-grease'.

The first systematic exposé of English food adulteration, published in 1820, was the work of German-born freelance scientist Friedrich Accum (1769–1838). A specialist in what one might call the science of everyday life, Accum had won modest fame as the man who brought gas-lighting to the streets of London and won a modest fortune from his textbooks and works on the manufacture of bread and beer.

Accum's *Treatise on the Adulterations of Food and Culinary Poisons* was a hard-hitting, 'name and shame' account of the current abuses of the food industry, which included:

- Adding red lead to re-colour fading cayenne pepper.
- 'Extending' white pepper with floor dust.
- Recycling used tea leaves for resale.
- Adding copper coins to pickles to produce a 'lively green'.

The first edition of 1,000 copies of the *Treatise* sold out in a month. But Accum had made powerful enemies who used his position as Librarian of the Royal Institution to engineer his disgrace and downfall. Faced with planted evidence and false testimony that he had cut expensive plates out of library books to sell them, Accum fled back to Germany.

Pulling no punches. The frontispiece from the first edition of Accum's exposé of food adulteration showed that he was quite literally in deadly earnest about the threat to human health.

The crusade against food adulteration stalled for thirty years until taken up by Thomas Wakley (1795–1862), editor of *The Lancet*. Wakley recruited his own in-house scientists, publishing the results of their analyses of common food items in a three-year campaign which showed that:

- Every one of 49 bread samples contained alum to whiten it.

- Of 29 samples of coffee, 28 contained ground acorns, mangel-wurzel or dried horse's blood.

- Tea was routinely bulked out with sloe, privet or sycamore leaves.

- Cocoa was 'extended' with brick dust, pepper with sand, mustard with flour and turmeric.

The more astute food manufacturers rapidly saw the market value of selling 'Pure and Unadulterated' foods and gave up the worst practices voluntarily. Mr Horniman, who pioneered the sale of tea in sealed, tamper-proof packets, became Britain's largest supplier.

In 1860 Britain enacted the world's first food purity law; but it was the Adulteration of Food, Drink and Drugs Act of 1872 that led to the general appointment of public analysts. Their efforts ensured that the public was henceforth only 'cheated rather than poisoned'.

DO YOU BANT?

Like Louis Pasteur and Captain Boycott, William Banting (1797–1878) achieved the unusual distinction of seeing his surname become an English verb – although 'banting' nowadays only survives in Swedish as the word for dieting.

Mr Banting by his mid-sixties stood 5 feet 5 inches and weighed 202 pounds. Worried at the onset of deafness, in August 1862 Banting consulted ear specialist Dr William Harvey of Soho Square, who diagnosed obesity as the cause. Harvey advised Banting to cut out bread, butter, milk, sugar, pork, potatoes, beans and beer and substitute meat, fish, fruit, non-root vegetables and dry toast.

Following the recommended diet Banting lost 12 inches off his waistline and 46 pounds in a year. Eager to spread the gospel according to Dr Harvey, Banting composed *A Letter on Corpulence Addressed to the Public.*

Written in simple, non-technical language, 1,000 copies were given away free by the author. In response to its success he gave away another 1,500. Then a third edition, priced at a shilling – the cost of a dozen daily papers – still sold 60,000 copies. The *Letter* was translated into French and German, while pirate editions circulated in the United States.

Banting maintained his weight loss and died aged 81. Dr Harvey, however, was defamed in the medical community, partly for straying out of his proper area of expertise, but mainly because he could provide no scientific explanation of how his diet actually worked.

✸ THE FIRST CELEBRITY CHEF ✸

Alexis Soyer (1809–58) never set out to become a founding father of army catering. Consider his notions for the artful management of a society dinner party:

> *I do not have the dessert placed on the table until ten or twenty*
> *minutes after the cloth is removed: this gives an opportunity*
> *for…guests to admire the beautiful Sèvres dessert plates,*
> *containing views of different French chateaux…a subject of*
> *conversation to those who have visited them. In the dessert*
> *I generally introduce some new importation such as bananas,*
> *sugar cane, American Lady apples, prickly pear etc. and these*
> *also give a subject for the gentlemen to talk about when the*
> *ladies have left, such as free trade, colonial policy etc.*

That Soyer's birthplace, Meaux-en-Brie, combined the names of both a celebrated mustard and a cheese was prophetic. Apprenticed to a cook at twelve, by the time he was 21 Soyer was second cook at the French foreign office. The revolution of 1830 cost him his job so he left for London and by 1837 was chef at the newly founded Reform Club. The hygienic, labour-saving kitchen Soyer designed at the Reform became one of the capital's off-beat tourist attractions, its state-of-the-art gas ovens a generation ahead of their time. Thereafter, his career went through various peaks and troughs:

- **1847** sets up a soup kitchen in Dublin to feed refugees from the potato famine.

- **1848** does the same for the poor of Spitalfields. Soyer then boosted his fortune by inventing a small 'magic' spirit stove for cooking dishes at the table, a patent relish and a 'cooling water…to quench the spark in the throat'.

- **1849** Soyer goes for the mass-market with *The Modern Housewife: Comprising Nearly 1,000 Receipts for the Economic and Judicious Preparation of Every Meal of the Day, with those of the Nursery and Sick-room.* It went into a second edition in a fortnight.

- **1851** Soyer opens a top-line establishment, *The Gastronomic Symposium of All Nations*, opposite the Great Exhibition in Hyde Park. It was a huge success – and lost him £7,000.

- **1854–5** Soyer bounces back with a monumental *History of Food in All Ages* and a *Shilling Cookery Book for the People*, which sold 110,000 copies in four months.

MILITARY MISSION

In 1855 Soyer, shocked by reports from the war in the Crimea of military mismanagement, volunteered to support Florence Nightingale's nursing mission. Once there, Soyer reorganized the victualling at three hospitals and took over the cooking for an entire division of the army. The 'cooking wagon' he devised became the official army field-stove for a century.

The master chef's Crimean experiences were turned to permanent account in Soyer's *Culinary Campaign, with the Plain Art of Cookery for Military and Civil Institutions.* Soyer went on to reform cooking at the

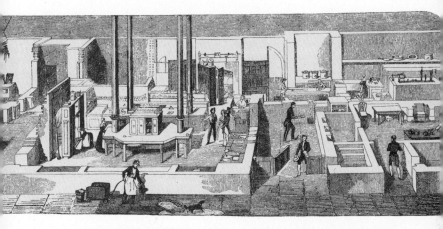

Ahead of its time. The kitchens designed by Alexis Soyer at the Reform Club featured a spacious layout, designed for optimal efficiency, with hygienic work-surfaces.

home army's hospitals and the government emigration commission and supervised the construction of a model military kitchen at London's Wellington Barracks.

Weakened by 'Crimean fever' and a riding accident, and exhausted by his catering crusade, Soyer died, not yet 50, leaving a personal estate of less than £1,500. In the words of Florence Nightingale:

> *His death is a great disaster. Others have studied cooking for the purpose of gourmandising, some for show but none for the purpose of cooking large quantities of food in the most nutritious manner for great numbers of men. He has no successor.*

✸ DOMESTIC GODDESS ✸

The name of 'Mrs Beeton' conjures up a formidable middle-aged matron, laying down domestic law for younger and lesser females. But she died aged just 29. Isabella Beeton (1836–65) grew up as the eldest of 21 children – a thorough grounding in household life. When she was 21 (and doubtless eager to escape home) she married ambitious publisher Samuel Beeton.

Isabella immediately set to work on *The Englishwoman's Domestic Magazine*, contributing monthly supplements; these were then reissued as *The Book of Household Management*.

PET PROJECT

This was entirely her project, pushed through despite the death of her second child while she put it together. As its title implies, Mrs Beeton's compendium contained far more than recipes, covering servants, budgets and the organization of housework with chapters on medical and even legal matters, 'with a history of the Origin, Properties and Uses of All things Connected with Home Life and Comfort'.

Careful readers would learn about everything from the cultivation of almonds and the migration of salmon to the place of sheep in poetry. Recipes, for anything from six to 60 diners, were presented systematically in terms of ingredients, method, costs, portions, seasonality and preparation time.

Though she had invited readers to send in their own favourite recipes, Isabella found most useless and instead used Eliza Acton's classic cookery book and other successful contemporary works, testing and amending their recipes as she thought fit.

Running to 1,296 pages *The Book of Household Management* weighed in at a hefty three pounds. For new and uncertain female recruits to Victorian England's rapidly expanding middle class it was a godsend. Published when the author was just 23, it sold 60,000 copies in its first year.

The year after Mrs Beeton's death, her husband's business crashed in the banking crisis of 1866. Ward Lock & Co. bought up his assets, including *The Book of Household Management*. By 1890 it had sold 500,000 copies. It has never been out of print since.

7

BELIEVE IT OR NOT

Religion is by no means a proper subject
of conversation in a mixed company.

PHILIP DORMER STANHOPE, EARL OF CHESTERFIELD,
LETTERS TO HIS SON, 1750

For a thousand years England was universally Catholic and then for centuries passionately Protestant. The central role of religion in England's history is therefore easily overlooked. Most of us know William Wilberforce as the man who abolished the slave trade – but not, perhaps, as the best-selling author of *Practical Christianity*, which went through 15 editions in 20 years.

This chapter explores some of the ways in which religion has framed belief and shaped behaviour.

FROM CULT TO CANONIZATION

For almost a thousand years Christian saints were created by popular acclaim rather than papal approval. The removal of a holy man's body from its grave for reburial in a church marked accept- ance of his sainthood, confirmed by pilgrimage to what had thus become a shrine. This cult of 'local heroes' was overseen by the bishop of each diocese. By the tenth century disputed claims began to be referred to the Pope.

ROME TAKES CHARGE

In 993 John XV became the first Pope to create a saint on his own authority. Beginning with Alexander III (reigned 1159–81), a succession of Popes trained in Church (canon) law established control over the making of saints by drawing up an officially approved list or 'canon' and establishing a formal process of investigating candidates for 'canonization'. By the time of Gregory IX (reigned 1227–41) papal approval was mandatory. In 1634 Urban VIII forbade the veneration of anyone not canonized by the church – unless their cult was at least a century old.

HOLY GROUND

More than 80 place names in England incorporate the name of a saint and more than half of those are in Cornwall.

England's first martyr, the Roman soldier St Alban, was converted by a priest on the run, changed clothes with him so he could escape and was arrested in his place. According to Bede, the eyes of Alban's executioner subsequently fell out of his head.

The Abbey founded in Alban's name by Offa of Mercia became one of the wealthiest in England and the nucleus of the city of St Albans.

Edmund the Martyr, King of East Anglia, was executed by Vikings in 870, either with arrows or by beheading. His body was later translated from Norfolk to Suffolk where Canute founded the abbey of Bury St Edmunds in his honour in 1020.

The remains of saints were often moved by monarchs from marginal locations to centres of power where they could do more good. Thus St Oswald was taken all the way from Tynemouth to Gloucester and St Judoc from Cornwall to Winchester.

Burying St Edmund. The entombment of the patron saint of Bury St Edmund's. On 14 November 1214 – St Edmund's Day – the barons met in the abbey to swear they would force King John to sign the Magna Carta.

✳ THE ONLY ENGLISH POPE ✳

The son of a poor man, Nicholas Breakspear was abandoned when his father became a monk at St Albans Abbey. Nicholas begged his way to France, entered the monastery of St Rufus, near Avignon, as a servant, and rose to become Abbot.

When his austere rule provoked a near revolt among his easy-going brethren, Pope Eugenius III intervened in person and decided that Nicholas deserved promotion rather than punishment.

Elevated to cardinal, Nicholas was sent to Scandinavia to reorganize the church hierarchy; this he did with such success that he was nicknamed 'The Apostle of the North' and marked out as the obvious successor to the throne of St Peter.

Elected Pope on Christmas Day, 1154, Nicholas took the name Adrian IV. A man of great learning and a magnetic preacher with a fine voice, Adrian found the papal territories beset by enemies on all sides and spent his entire reign playing off one against another.

When a cardinal was attacked on the streets of Rome itself Adrian did something no previous Pope had ever dared to do and put the Eternal City under interdict – suspending the normal life of the Church. This killed off the profitable pilgrimage trade and soon brought the Romans to heel, though later he had to flee and spent the rest of his life on the move, before dying in 1159.

In retrospect the brief but eventful reign of Adrian IV is remembered for starting a long-running feud with the powerful Holy Roman Emperor, Frederick Barbarossa, and authorizing Henry II of England to conquer Ireland so that he could reform its 'rough and ignorant people'. This permission was only supposed to last for the king's lifetime – a condition subsequent English monarchs conveniently ignored.

Nicholas Breakspear never returned to his native land after leaving it in his youth and no medieval Pope ever visited England either.

✴ MONUMENT TO MARTYRDOM ✴

The first book to make its way into any Tudor household that could afford one would be the Bible. The second would be John Foxe's *Book of Martyrs*. This told the stories – in gory detail and with vivid illustrations – of the persecution and sufferings of those who had died for the Protestant cause, especially the 300 executed during the reign of 'Bloody Mary'.

Born to a poor family, John Foxe (1516–87) nevertheless seemed set for an academic career at Oxford when his strongly Protestant convictions cut that short. With the accession of Mary Tudor in 1553 Foxe fled abroad and, despite great poverty, diligently gathered material for his great epic.

Written first in Latin and then rendered into English 'for the good of the country and the information of the multitude', it was published in 1563 as the *Actes and Monuments of these Latter Perilous Days Touching matters of the Church* but became instantly known as the *Book of Martyrs*. Its success was considerable:

- A second, much improved edition was published in 1570 in two volumes, of 934 and 1,378 pages respectively.

- The Convocation of the Church of England ordered that a copy should be placed in every cathedral and in the home of every bishop and deacon.

- Hundreds of parish churches bought their own copy and thousands of clergymen used it as a source for their sermons.

- Further editions appeared in 1576 and 1583 and, after Foxe's death, five more between 1596 and 1684.

Tarnished by credulousness and partiality in modern eyes, Foxe nevertheless commands respect for the courage of his convictions:

Fiery exit. Dampened wood enabled the more fortunate martyrs to die of smoke inhalation before the actual flames reached them. Under Elizabeth, Jesuit priests were more often hanged, drawn and quartered than burned.

- He refused celibacy, costing him his college fellowship.

- He refused to wear a surplice, costing him a profitable office in the church he stoutly defended.

- In 1563 he worked fearlessly to comfort victims of the plague.

- Later he petitioned the queen herself to reprieve his religious archenemies, the Jesuits, from execution.

Foxe was, in the words of a later authority, 'appallingly industrious' but 'neither scrupulous nor scholarly'. None of which prevented the *Book of Martyrs* from becoming the inspirational handbook of popular Protestantism.

✳ WHAT WERE PURITANS? ✳

Nowadays virtually a term of abuse, the word 'Puritan', first recorded in 1569, was for a century central to the debate on English religious identity.

Puritans were originally members of the Church of England who wanted it to be 'purer' and free from surviving Catholic traditions, ranging from the physical layout of the church to the style of worship. Specifically, they objected to:

- Having a screen between the congregation in the nave and the priest in the chancel.

- The priest wearing a surplice and fine vestments of silk or embroidery.

- The use of the ring in marriage.

- Making the sign of the cross.

- Painted or carved images of the Virgin Mary and saints.

They wanted to replace railed-off altars decorated with crosses and candles with plain tables.

Puritans especially valued sermons above ceremonies and esteemed learned and skilful preachers.

In their personal lives, in their families and at work Puritans looked to be sober, industrious and orderly. They valued prayer and discussion of religious matters. Many wrote diaries to keep a record of their deeds and thoughts as a way of checking that they were living up to 'godly' standards.

Support for Puritanism was especially strong in eastern England and London, the most prosperous and literate parts of the nation. Cambridge University in particular produced many Puritan preachers.

Puritans were never a single body with a single viewpoint. The most moderate wanted no more than the reform of worship. Later, more radical Puritans wanted to replace bishops with government by senior members of congregations (presbyters) meeting periodically as synods or by a church in which every congregation was independent. Puritans of both types desired a 'reformation of manners' to create a godly, rather than a sinful society. The most extreme Puritans, known as sectaries, believed the end of the world was near.

RISE...

Puritans were alarmed by the accession of Charles I, who married a French Catholic queen and appointed the traditionalist William Laud as Archbishop of Canterbury to re-establish more elaborate forms of worship.

This alienated not only Puritans but also many mainstream Anglicans who were branded as such. During the 1630s at least 20,000 left for the American colonies in a 'Great Migration' for religious freedom.

Puritan domination of Parliament during the Civil War led to the abolition of bishops, rejection of the *Book of Common Prayer* in 1645 and Laud's execution. Church monuments and stained glass were systematically destroyed.

...AND FALL

The collapse of the Anglican order after the execution of Charles I in 1649 left the Puritans divided about how to replace it. Presbyterians wanted a state church on Scottish lines. Independents wanted each congregation to be autonomous. Having already closed down London's theatres and banned animal-baiting, the Puritan-dominated government also suppressed the celebration of Christmas.

The breakdown of state censorship led to the publication of thousands of pamphlets airing critical ideas. This protest against the prohibition of Christmas also condemned onerous taxes and the banning of brewing strong ale for the festive season.

The Restoration of the monarchy in 1660 was accompanied by an Anglican backlash that marginalized the Puritans.

Puritanism as an ethos remained an enduring strand in English life, manifested in admiration for personal integrity, frugality and industriousness, in a distaste for artistic excess, in sexual repressiveness and in the boredom of an 'English Sunday', the last of which horrified Continental visitors.

✠ THE WITCHCRAFT CRAZE ✠

...many persons of both sexes, unmindful of their own salvation and straying from the Catholic faith, have abandoned themselves to devils...and by their incantations, spells, conjurations and accursed charms and crafts, enormities and horrid offences, have slain infants yet in the mother's womb...

POPE INNOCENT VIII, 1484

Witches, surprised by a servant, flee her employer's mansion in the company of their master, Satan. By the time this print was produced in the late seventeenth century credence in witches was fading, especially among the educated.

Accusations of witchcraft were known but rare in medieval Europe. That changed after 1484 when Pope Innocent VIII appointed two friars, Henry Kramer and James Spenger, as Inquisitors into a field in which they claimed to have unrivalled expertise as authors of the *Malleus Maleficarum* (*Hammer of Evildoing*).

Allegedly based on eyewitness accounts and the confessions of witches themselves, this preposterous fabrication of falsehoods and titillation was hailed as the definitive authority on witchcraft. For the next two centuries witchcraft became a European obsession.

THE DEVIL'S GEOGRAPHY

The distribution of witchcraft accusations, trials and executions was dramatically uneven, ranging from virulent in Iceland (where 90 per cent of the accused were *men*) and in Switzerland (where the last European execution for witchcraft took place in 1786) to virtually unknown in Ireland, Spain or southern Italy – all areas in which the authority of the Catholic Church was undisturbed by Protestantism.

In England the fear of witches took half a century to catch on, emerging, perhaps significantly, around the time of the Dissolution of the Monasteries. Witchcraft became a felony in English law in 1542 and a capital offence in 1563.

Scottish law allowed torture, which may explain why during the sixteenth century there were 1,000 executions for witchcraft in Scotland as opposed to 500 in England, with its much bigger population. And within England itself the distribution was very uneven, with over 400 cases in Essex, but just 17 in Sussex.

GUILT AND INNOCENCE

In England overall three-quarters of accused witches were acquitted. Accusations were routinely dismissed on evidence of good character from supportive witnesses – usually four to eight. In Essex, the outcome of about three-quarters of cases is known in detail. Slightly under half resulted in guilty verdicts; of those just over half were executed (by hanging, not burning). Thirty-six more died of fever in gaol – usually taken as God's visitation on the unrighteous. Execution was more likely when witchcraft was linked with heresy, poisoning, treason or murder.

Sceptical observers saw that witchcraft accusations not only poisoned communities but also damaged faith in conventional medicine:

> *My question is not whether there be witches or nay; but whether they can do such marvellous works as are imputed to them…. I am sorry and ashamed to see how many die, that being said to be bewitched, only seek for magical cures, whom wholesome diet and good medicines would have recovered.*

REGINALD SCOT, *THE DISCOVERY OF WITCHCRAFT*, 1584

WHY WITCHES?

Historians have suggested a sociological explanation for the witchcraft craze in England.

- The Dissolution of the Monasteries in the 1530s removed a powerful instrument for damping down social discontent and relieving hardship.

- A century of unprecedented religious turmoil, population growth and inflation pushed many to the edge of survival.

- Personal crises could be exorcized by victimizing the vulnerable.

- Significantly, witchcraft accusations peaked in the 1580s and 1590s against a background of bad harvests.

Women, who accounted for six out of seven of those accused of witchcraft – especially old, single women without husbands or children to defend them – would traditionally have had a claim on the charity of

DEMISE OF A DELUSION

The first witchcraft execution in colonial America was not until 1647 – long after the peak of the witch-craze in Europe.

The Salem trials of 1692 are notorious but witchcraft was a very minor matter in America compared with Europe.

The last execution for witchcraft in England was in 1686 in Exeter and the last trial held in 1712.

Laws against witchcraft were repealed in 1736 and replaced by a law against 'pretended witchcraft', which was treated as a form of confidence trick, punishable by a year's imprisonment.

The last person convicted under the 1735 Act was Jane Rebecca Yorke of Forest Gate, London – in 1944.

their community but, it is argued, in a harsh climate of falling real incomes and longer working hours, they were victimized because their poverty and neglect was a reproach to their neighbours.

The disorders of the civil wars led to a localized revival of witch-hunting in Puritan East Anglia, led by a self-appointed 'Witch-Finder General', Matthew Hopkins of Manningtree, Essex.

Hopkins had more than 200 victims executed between 1645 and 1647 before being himself denounced and hanged for sorcery.

✳ TYING THE KNOT ✳

Marriage is popular because it combines the maximum
of temptation with the maximum of opportunity.

GEORGE BERNARD SHAW, *MAN AND SUPERMAN*, 1903

Marriage is both an event and a condition. What follows is about getting married, rather than being married – a much larger topic, as any one who is (or has been) married certainly knows.

BEARING WITNESS

Weddings have always been communal acts, witnessed by the wider community:

- Pope Alexander III (1159–81) decreed that marriage vows should be made before witnesses, preferably *outside* the door of the parish church. This implies reliance on collective memory rather than written records because lower clergy were often still illiterate.

SETTING THE DATE

Finding the right day for the ceremony wasn't always easy:

In the Middle Ages marriage was forbidden during Advent, Lent, Rogationtide and on major holy days – amounting to roughly half the days in the year.

Parish registers show Lent marriages were still effectively prohibited in Protestant England until the nineteenth century.

August – harvest month – was too busy for weddings.

Pregnancy was often the key factor in organizing preparations for the actual marriage ceremony. As late as 1800 over half of all first births were conceived outside marriage.

- Vows were to be in the local language, not in Latin, so that all could understand.

- If it could be established in court that a marriage had never been consummated it could be nullified – hence the usual presence of witnesses at the first bedding of a newly married couple.

- Medieval society had no minimum age for marriage so legally binding betrothal promises and marriage vows were exchanged between children. Because their purpose was to ensure succession to lands and titles, when such events took place between aristocratic families they were usually recorded in writing.

From 1538 marriages in England had to be recorded in the parish register; however, this was often done irregularly during periods of religious change, like the reigns of Edward VI and Mary, or the civil wars.

The *Book of Common Prayer*, composed by Thomas Cranmer (England's first married Archbishop), added another justification for marriage, apart from procreation: that the couple might enjoy one another.

FLEET MARRIAGES

In the eighteenth century a notorious scandal developed with the performance of 'Fleet marriages' in private 'chapels' near London's Fleet Prison for debtors, which usually contained several clergy (real or fake) down on their luck.

Ceremonies were often conducted secretly and often when one or both parties was drunk. This led to some alarming mismatches between rich young men out for a good time and 'ladies of pleasure' deciding it was time to be good.

Casual nuptials. A down-at-heel clergyman weds a hasty couple in front of a crowd of costermongers to general amusement; no altar, no prayer book and no written record. The building at the rear is the Royal Exchange as rebuilt after the Great Fire of 1666.

In 1757 'Fleet marriages' were brought to an end by 'Lord Hardwicke's Act', promoted by the Lord Chancellor of the day. He was much less concerned about the morality of clandestine marriages than about their potential effect on the family business of aristocrats – passing on inherited wealth. It is estimated that in the half century before Hardwicke's Act some 200,000–300,000 'Fleet marriages' were performed. Most were *not* for drunken toffs but for the young and the poor – in part because they could be accomplished before parents or employers could intervene, and in part because they were cheaper.

Lord Hardwicke's Act required that:

- Marriage must be preceded by the calling of banns (to allow for hangovers to clear or objections to be made) or by the granting of a written licence; minors had to have the permission of parents or guardians.

- Marriages must be solemnized in a church, according to the *Book of Common Prayer*, and in a parish where one of the parties was resident.

- A record of the marriage had to be kept in a dedicated book, the entries being signed by parties and witnesses.

Jews and Quakers were exempted from Hardwicke's Act. Dissenters (Baptists, Congregationalists and so forth) were not exempted until 1836, when they were permitted to marry in their own chapels or by civil contract. Catholics were similarly disadvantaged.

The later Marriage Act of 1836 established superintendent registrars of births, deaths and marriages – they had the duty of registering all marriages and licensing non-Anglican premises. Register Offices were also established for marriage without a religious ceremony.

RACE TO THE ALTAR?

Parish registers show that since the sixteenth century the average age of marriage in England has been in the mid-twenties. At least one in six people in the sixteenth and seventeenth centuries never married; chief among these were seamen and domestic servants.

Industrialization widened the range of employment and the mobility of the population, lowering the average age of marriage. Marriage young was especially common where men reached their peak earnings (related to physical strength) early, as in mining; waiting on an inheritance or serving out an apprenticeship delayed marriage. So, in the 1880s most miners were married by 24 while the average for men in 'the professions' was 30.

WEARING WHITE

White wedding dresses are a late Victorian introduction. Wedding photographs from the early twentieth century show that the custom caught on only gradually. It was probably general by the inter-war period – when the proportion of virgin brides was higher than ever before or since.

MARRIAGE STAKES

Choosing the right match could be critical, especially if you were a wealthy woman:

Until the nineteenth century, marriage in England brought a husband total rights over a wife's property and earnings – hence the preoccupation with wealthy heiresses in many plays and novels.

It was, however, possible for a bride's family to impose legal restrictions on her dowry as part of a marriage settlement – e.g., guaranteeing her an annual sum for her personal use.

The Married Womens' Property Act (1870) recognized the principle that women might retain control over their own property but was flawed and ineffective in practice.

The Married Women's Property Act (1882) was a legal landmark, allowing wives to acquire, hold, use and dispose of their separate property as freely as if unmarried and with the same legal protections.

FAMILY SIZE

Family sizes have varied widely according to region, class, occupation, ethnicity and religion. Women born between 1771 and 1831 bore an average of six children (not all of whom were likely to have survived). By the 1880s this had fallen to three, and in the generation after that to two.

There were very large families in late Victorian Britain, of course: indeed, 10 per cent had ten children or more. However, since this 10 per cent accounted for 25 per cent of all children, there must have been far more smaller families than large ones.

NAME GAME

Among the propertied classes it was common when a family had produced only daughters for the son-in-law who married the eldest and heiress to change his surname to hers to perpetuate the family name.

DESERTION, DEATH AND DIVORCE

Because divorce was effectively unattainable for most of the population, marriages among the poor were traditionally 'dissolved' simply by desertion. This was far less possible for their 'betters', who had property at stake.

Nowadays the duration of a marriage largely depends on whether or not it ends in divorce. In the past the key factor was death. In the 1730s, for example, a quarter of all marriages lasted less than ten years; death in or after childbirth was probably the most common cause of this. At the same time, only a sixth of marriages lasted more than 40 years.

By the 1880s the proportion of marriages ending within ten years had fallen to one seventh while more than a third lasted more than 40 years.

One consequence of the disruption of marriage by death was the existence of a large category of widows and widowers. In the sixteenth century about 30 per cent of marriages included at least one partner who was a widower or widow.

By the seventeenth century, Church of England courts could grant separations but these did not entitle people to remarry. This was to change over time:

- In 1670 Lord Roos obtained a private Act of Parliament enabling him to remarry after obtaining a church decree of separation.

- Subsequently, this procedure also required a successful prosecution against one's partner for 'criminal conversation' (adultery).

- Between the 1780s and the 1840s divorces via this procedure averaged four per year.

- The entire number of divorces known from 1700 up to 1857 amounts to only 330.

- In 1857 English church courts lost their jurisdiction over marriage and a Divorce Court was established with secular procedures.
- After each further liberalization of divorce laws (1923, 1937, 1969) the number of divorces increased substantially.
- The average annual number of divorces in the period just before the First World War was 600; by the 1930s, 4,000; and by the 1940s, 30,000.

NANNY TO THE NATION

When Jane Austen went to live in Bath she was a literary unknown, whose family had to hunt hard for tolerable lodgings. Hannah More (1745–1833), on the other hand, came as an established celebrity to live on Great Pulteney Street, the most fashionable address in the city.

LITERARY LAUNCH

Born to a Bristolian family of teachers, Hannah More would come to take the entire nation as her classroom and the moral high ground as her personal territory.

- **1762** More's first work, *The Search after Happiness*, a didactic drama for her pupils, is published when she was just 17.
- **1774** *The Search for Happiness* is republished in London, making her a national name.
- **1775** David Garrick, the leading theatrical talent of the century, staged her play, *The Inflexible Captive*, at Bath's Theatre Royal.

Sitting pretty. The pen and inkstand barely hint at Hannah More's voluminous output of publications while her plush accoutrements testify to their reward.

- **1779** More is included in a group portrait of *The Nine Living Muses of Great Britain.*

- **1780s** More has become an earnest evangelical and a supporter of the anti-slavery movement.

Moving in the highest cultural circles, Hannah More was well placed to compose her *Thoughts on the Importance of the Manners of the Great to General Society*. Published in 1788, this went to a second printing, which sold out in six days and a third which went in four *hours*. Her *Estimate of the Religion of the Fashionable World* ran to five editions.

DEFENDER OF THE FAITH

The outbreak of revolution in France – and the fear of revolution in England – led More to stop writing tomes for toffs in favour of pamphlets for plebs, defending orthodox religion and the established social order.

More's 'Cheap Repository Tracts' sold 700,000 copies within the first four months of their appearance, and more than 2,000,000 in the first year. Between 1795 and 1798, 114 were published, of which 49 she wrote herself. In 1799 the task was taken over by the newly established Religious Tract Society and More returned to type with her *Strictures on the Modern System of Female Education. Practical Piety* went to 12 editions in a decade, *Moral Sketches* to seven in a couple of years.

When More died at the age of 88 she left some £30,000 to good causes. A four-volume memoir of her life and letters appeared within a year – quite a tribute to a self-educated female from the lower end of the provincial middle classes.

ENGLAND'S MOST POPULAR PREACHER

John Donne won royal favour not because he was a great poet but because he was a great preacher. John Wesley won popular acclaim by preaching some 40,000 sermons. Both of them were Oxford men but the pulpit star of Victoria's reign was an agricultural college dropout.

Charles Haddon Spurgeon (1834–92) preached his first sermon aged 16, was a Baptist pastor at 18, famous at 20 and by 22 was the most popular preacher in Britain.

Ten thousand people came to hear him at the music hall in Surrey Gardens. Then, in 1861, Spurgeon took possession of the Metropolitan Tabernacle at Newington Causeway. Purpose-built for him at a cost of £31,000, this monster preaching-box could hold a regular congregation of 6,000 and had a lecture-room for 900 and a schoolhouse for 1,000. Spurgeon's empire also included a pastor's college at Camberwell, an orphanage and a prolific programme of pamphlet publishing.

When Spurgeon chose to retire at 45 he was presented with a testimonial of £6,263. Five years after Spurgeon's death more than 2,500 of his sermons were still on sale.

8

ENGLAND ABROAD

And what should they know of England
who only England know?

RUDYARD KIPLING, *THE ENGLISH FLAG*, 1891

This final chapter suggests that not only are the exploits of empire now forgotten but so, too, are the failures and false starts which might have made it very different from what it was.

✳ IMMORTALS IGNORED ✳

NAPIER

In Trafalgar Square stand two statues, 20 feet high but almost universally ignored. One is of Sir Charles Napier (1782–1853), who joined the army at 12, was wounded eight times during the Peninsular War and conquered the Indian frontier province of Sind in 1841–43. Popular myth credited him with sending a one-word Latin despatch – 'Peccavi', meaning 'I have sinned' (Sind).

Following his own maxim that 'the best way to quiet a country is a good thrashing, followed by great kindness', Napier imposed an effective administration, suppressed the custom of sati (widow-burning) and built the harbour at Karachi; hence the scroll his statue holds, symbolizing good governance. He died of a chill caught as a pall-bearer at the Duke of Wellington's funeral.

Of fiery temper, Napier was also of royal lineage, being the great-great-grandson of Charles II. Also a cousin of the radical Charles James Fox, Napier sympathized with the travails of the working classes and successfully policed the North of England during the Chartist tensions of 1839-40, preventing disorders.

Napier's statue was paid for with pennies from private soldiers. Sculptor George Ganon Adams took great liberties with his appearance, leaving off his thick-lensed spectacles, stuffing his bushy beard into his collar and smoothing out his hooked nose. Napier in New Zealand is named in the general's honour.

HAVELOCK

Napier's companion in Trafalgar Square, Sir Henry Havelock (1795–1857), became a hero in his last year of life, having taken 23 years to reach captain.

When part of the Indian army mutinied in 1857, Havelock was ordered to relieve the besieged garrison at Cawnpore and won it with a ruse of Fredrick the Great, sending just 18 crack cavalrymen against 5,000 rebels and successfully provoking them into a devastating ambush.

Pressing on to besieged Lucknow, Havelock, although over 60, personally led the charge through to the Residency but died of dysentery before the rebels were finally defeated. Havelock therefore never received the baronetcy and pension of £1,000 a year awarded by a grateful nation.

As Havelock was buried in India, his statue was the first in London to be modelled from a photograph.

OUTRAM

The statue of Sir James Outram (1803–63) stands in Embankment Gardens. After Havelock's death at Lucknow, Outram took charge, holding out for three months against a besieging army of 130,000 with a garrison of just 5,000. Also awarded a baronetcy and £1,000 a year, Outram was buried in Westminster Abbey.

Right *An officer at 16, Outram served his early years on the jungle frontier of British India. In ten years he killed 191 tigers, 25 bears and 15 leopards.*

Opposite *Havelock's statue was unveiled in 1861 without ceremony. Sculptor William Behnes went bankrupt that year and was found drunk and dying in the gutter in 1864 with just threepence in his pockets.*

FRERE

Next to Outram stands Sir Bartle Frere (1815–84). In Sind the multilingual Frere built more than 6,000 miles of roads, founded schools and colleges, improved public sanitation and issued India's first printed postage stamps. Frere went on to suppress Zanzibar's ancient slave market but as governor of Cape Colony was blamed for the failures of the Zulu War and recalled.

GORDON

Outside the Ministry of Defence stands the brooding figure of General Charles George Gordon (1832–85).

Sherlock Holmes had two portraits on his study wall: one was of Queen Victoria, the other of General Gordon. Gordon trained as an engineer, thoroughly enjoyed the terrible hardships of the Crimean War and became a national hero during the Taiping rebellion in China for transforming 3,000 unruly mercenaries and peasants into an 'Ever Victorious Army'. Gordon came through without a scratch, returning home as 'Chinese Gordon'.

Gordon as Governor-General of Sudan, 1880. Gordon had lived a charmed life in the Crimea and China, apparently invulnerable to shot and shell. However, after his death in Khartoum his head was spiked on a pole in the camp of the Mahdi.

Appointed governor of the Sudan, Gordon battled to suppress the slave trade and later talked the Chinese out of an 'idiotic' war against Russia, served as governor of Mauritius, reported on racial unrest in Basutoland, and wrote a book on the sacred geography of the Bible.

When Khartoum was threatened by a massive jihad led by the mystic Mahdi, Gordon was sent to evacuate its Egyptian garrison and European residents. Instead he chose to fortify and fight. After defying the Mahdi for several months, Gordon and the defenders were massacred. A relief force, commanded by General Wolseley, arrived two days too late.

DRIVEN BY DUTY

Empire may seem irrelevant – even immoral – to modern eyes, but its heroes still merit respect for their integrity as well as their personal courage and professionalism.

As Commander-in-Chief of India, Napier resigned in protest against pay cuts imposed on the native troops. Had he been heeded there might have been no mutiny in 1857.

A devout Christian, Havelock scorned ridicule to organize Bible classes and coffee houses for his men, who became known as 'Havelock's Saints'.

Outram opposed the conquest of Sind and gave his £3,000 prize money to Indian charities.

'Chinese Gordon' spent a decade in obscurity building useless fortifications along the Thames and donating most of his salary to support a school for street urchins.

The son of a carpenter, Campbell supported his father and sister and took 40 years of frugal service to free himself of debt and reach the rank of colonel.

Field Marshal Roberts died on active service at 82, visiting Indian troops on the Western Front.

During the Boer War, Field Marshal White, aged 65, successfully commanded the defence of Ladysmith during a siege of 118 days.

CAMPBELL

At Waterloo Place stands the statue of Sir Colin Campbell (1792–1863), another late career hero. During the Crimean War, Campbell led the Highland Brigade at the storming of Alma and at Balaclava commanded the original 'Thin Red Line' that saw off a charge of Russian heavy cavalry.

As commander-in-chief during the Indian rebellion, Campbell led the largest British field army since Waterloo to the relief of Lucknow. Baron Marochetti's statue shows Campbell wearing the patrol jacket and cord breeches in which he fought his last campaign.

BURGOYNE

Campbell's companion on Waterloo Place is Field Marshal Sir John Fox Burgoyne (1782–1871), a soldier for almost 70 years. The illegitimate son of a general and a singer, he became a demolitions expert. Happily, he spent much of his career constructively, building bridges, laying sewers, administering relief during the Irish famine, judging the military exhibits at the Great Exhibition, and serving as Constable of the Tower of London.

WOLSELEY

Horseguards Parade is overlooked by the equestrian statues of two more fighting generals. One statue is of Field Marshal Garnet Wolseley (1833–1913), who lost an eye in the Crimea but was still the first soldier to get through at Lucknow with Campbell's final relief force. He conquered the Ashanti in West Africa, fought in the Zulu War and in a meticulously planned desert night attack defeated the forces of the Mahdi at Tel-el-Kebir when commanding the expedition to relieve General Gordon. He ended his career as Commander-in-Chief.

Wolseley's *Soldier's Pocket Book* contained advice on topics as diverse as surveying, snakebite and singing, and became a military classic. 'All Sir Garnet' became the regular expression for the ultimate in organization and efficiency. Giving your 'Sir Garnet' meant pledging absolute truth and commitment. Guyed by Gilbert and Sullivan on stage as 'the very model of a modern major-general', he was.

ROBERTS

Flanking Wolseley is pint-sized (5 feet 3 inches) 'Bobs' – Field Marshal Frederick Sleigh Roberts, first Earl Roberts of Kandahar, Pretoria and Waterford (1832–1914) – who was awarded the Victoria Cross 'for habitual disregard of danger'.

During the 1857 uprising Roberts took part in the siege of Delhi and the relief of Lucknow and captured a rebel standard. During the second Afghan War he led a column of 10,000 on an epic three-week march from Kabul to relieve Kandahar. Having served as Commander-in-Chief of the Indian army, he was appointed Commander-in-Chief of British forces during the Boer War, reversing the tide of defeats.

Modest, chivalrous and charming, Roberts was adored by the public. He was also a first-class rider, huntsman and polo player, and in time his horse, Volonel, became almost as famous as its owner.

Named after an Assamese chief Roberts had defeated, Volonel was little more than a pony but its stamina in the Afghan campaign led Queen Victoria to insist that it be awarded the Kabul to Kandahar Star and the Afghan War Medal with four clasps. Almost 20 years later Roberts rode Volonel when he headed the colonial contingents in the procession to mark Victoria's Diamond Jubilee in 1897. The horse was eventually buried at Chelsea Hospital.

Charles Furse's painting of Lord Roberts on Volonel, entitled 41 Years in India, *appears to have taken some licence with the horse – though it is shown as large and white, in fact it was 'a spirited Arab grey' not much bigger than a pony.*

WHITE

An equestrian statue of Field Marshal Sir George White V.C. O.M. (1835–1912) stands isolated on Portland Place. White took 26 years to become a major, then won the Victoria Cross serving under Roberts in the Second Afghan War of 1879–80. Thereafter he advanced rapidly to become Commander-in-Chief of the Indian army.

CINDERELLA OF THE EMPIRE

When Charles II married the Portuguese princess Catherine of Braganza in 1661 he acquired two important territories. One of these, Bombay, was half a year away by ship; the other, Tangier, could be reached from England in less than a fortnight.

PORT WITH POTENTIAL

Located on the Strait of Gibraltar, Tangier had been in Portuguese hands for almost two centuries but was entirely surrounded by the hostile kingdom of Morocco. The British nevertheless saw it as a potential naval base, with the additional prospect of trade in corn, hides and oils and, more alluringly, in copper, gold and fine horses. Poised between the Atlantic and the Mediterranean, Tangier seemed ideal for observing – and attacking – the main bases of Britain's rivals at Cadiz and Toulon. Admiralty bureaucrat Samuel Pepys recorded in his celebrated diary that Tangier was: 'likely to be the most considerable place the King of England hath in the world'.

A POPULATION PROBLEM

When the Portuguese population of Tangier left, there was the issue of how to populate the new possession. One suggestion was to send out all first offenders appearing before magistrates. Another was to relocate a third of the population of Scotland.

In the event the government settled for a mixed bag including criminals and political dissidents. Four thousand troops were sent out and set to work building a massive mole to make a safe anchorage and a complex of landward walls and forts. Later they were joined by skilled workmen from Yorkshire, for whom a dormitory suburb (called Whitby) was created.

A VIEW OF THE COLONY

In 1669 Bohemian engraver Wenceslaus Hollar produced detailed depictions of Tangier, marking in such features as 'the market place', 'the bowling green' and 'the Irish battery'.

By the 1670s there were almost as many civilian settlers as there were soldiers, including some 500 women and children. There was an Anglican church, a library, a mayor and aldermen and a network of streets with English names.

The mole by then stretched out 457 yards into the sea, was 100 feet wide and 18 feet high, with 26 cannon on one side and two batteries of 'great gunnes' on the other. When completed in 1677 the mole had absorbed 170,000 tons of rock and measured 3,000,000 cubic feet in volume. Maintaining the colony cost just short of £90,000 a year – more than all the home garrisons added together.

DOOMED TO FAILURE?

It is surprising that the enterprise lasted even as long as it did. The garrison was always heavily outnumbered by the Moors, who, despite periodic truces, were determined to recapture the city. When 500 troops made an exploratory sally out of the town defences in 1664, just nine returned alive. Disease and desertion claimed half the original complement of troops within two years. Control over the hinterland was never sufficient to guarantee supplies of fresh food or even water.

There were other problems. Imported provisions were three times the price they would have been in England and often rotten by the time they arrived. Pay was sometimes two years in arrears. As a result, in 1677 an outright mutiny had to be suppressed.

END GAME

In 1679 a blockade was imposed by a new Moroccan king, the iron-willed Moulay Ismail I, who had created a fresh strike force of freed slaves armed with European weapons. Three forts were lost, hundreds of troops killed and 57 taken as slaves. The British garrison, hastily reinforced, managed to fend off the immediate danger, despite six governors coming and going in the space of two years.

Charles II tried secretly to sell Tangier to France and then back to Portugal, but neither were interested. In 1683 a fleet was sent to carry out an evacuation.

LEGACY

Tangier was finally evacuated in 1684 and its fortifications blown up. The mole, which had cost £340,000, was destroyed to prevent the French or Spanish using the anchorage.

A SHOCKING STATE OF AFFAIRS

The fleet sent by Charles II to evacuate Tangier was accompanied by Samuel Pepys, who was appalled by the state of the settlement: 'Never was any town governed in all matters both public and private as this place has been…an excrescence of the earth and nothing but vice in the whole place of all sorts, for swearing, cursing, drinking and whoring.'

Charles II ordered that newly minted coins be buried deep in the wreckage of the town 'which haply, many centuries hence when other memory of it shall be lost, may declare to succeeding ages that place was once a member of the British empire.'

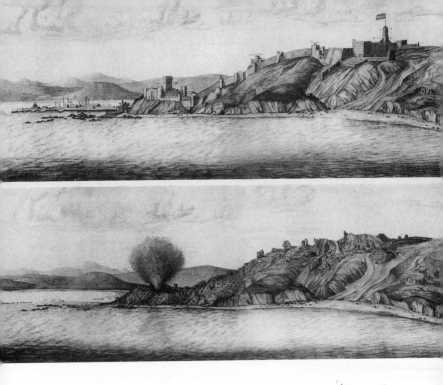

Scarcely 'Paradise Lost' – even when its fortifications were secure (top) many of its garrison regarded Tangier as a hell-hole. To deny it to others Tangier was systematically slighted (above) before its abandonment in 1684.

The exultant Ismail repossessed a ruin and, undismayed, reigned for another 40 years, fathering an alleged 700 sons and countless daughters.

The Tangier Regiment returned home. Many amalgamations later it has become part of the Princess of Wales's Royal Regiment, the senior English infantry regiment and the most highly decorated, with the oldest battle honour in the army – Tangier. The sole British legacy to Morocco has become its national drink – a nice cup of tea.

�֎ GARRISONS, GIN AND GRAVY ✶

Nowadays the English account for more than 60 per cent of foreign visitors to the second largest of the Balearic islands, Minorca. Few, however, are probably aware that for almost a century Minorca *was* British. Captured from Spain in 1708 during the War of Spanish Succession, its possession by the English was confirmed in 1713 by the Treaty of Utrecht, which also confirmed English possession of Gibraltar.

ENGLISH IMPRINT

An energetic governor, Richard Kane, set about developing the island's potential by draining swamplands and introducing Friesian cattle, thus giving birth to Minorca's now celebrated cheese-making industry.

Kane also built the first road across the island, providing a direct link between the two major settlements of Ciudadela and Port Mahon. To the annoyance of the locals, the seat of island government was transferred from the former to the latter, which overlooked the second largest natural harbour in the world. Perhaps they were mollified by another English innovation – the art of distilling gin.

Fort Marlborough, named for the hero of the recent war, was built to house a garrison. What is now Es Castell was known, rather unimaginatively, as Georgetown, in honour of the king. New buildings across the island featured distinctively English architectural features like bow windows and fanlight doors.

SHAME AND GLORY

The Seven Years War started in 1763 with a French attack on Port Mahon. The British fleet sent to confront them, under the experienced Admiral John Byng, was hastily prepared and inadequate to the task. Byng was dismayed to find the French already landed in strength. Uncertain how to proceed he was persuaded to abandon the garrison to its fate.

The commander of the besieged garrison was a veteran of 84, William Blakeney, who had taken until he was 65 to reach colonel but now proved the hero of the hour. At the head of a skeleton force made up largely of invalids and cripples, he held out for 70 days.

In recognition of his gallantry the French agreed that, in return for surrender, Blakeney could evacuate his men rather than having them taken prisoners of war. Blakeney was showered with honours – the Order of the Bath, a peerage, a statue in Dublin and, eventually, burial in Westminster Abbey.

But someone had to take the blame for losing a major British naval base. Byng was court-martialled, found guilty of neglect of duty and shot on his own ship. Byng's execution was regarded by his fellow officers as a shameful sacrifice made by an embarrassed government in need of a scapegoat.

The French philosopher Voltaire observed that in England it was apparently the custom to shoot an admiral from time to time 'to encourage the others'.

Like father, unlike son. Luckless Admiral Byng had the misfortune of being the son of a copper-bottomed naval hero, who had helped capture Gibraltar and annihilated a Spanish fleet.

REPRISE

Britain regained control of Minorca in 1763 at the end of the Seven Years War, before losing it again in 1782 when Spain joined in the closing stages of the American War of Independence. There was another brief British occupation between 1798 and 1802, during the war against revolutionary France.

LEGACY

In the long run the main benefit of British rule for the Minorcans was that their occupiers didn't care what language they spoke. On the Spanish mainland the government suppressed regional languages such as Catalan in favour of the Castilian spoken in the capital. On Minorca the local language, Menorquí, was allowed to flourish.

SAUCE OF PRIDE

The triumphant French commander, the Duc de Richelieu, celebrated his victory by having his chef concoct a new sauce in honour of the capture of Port Mahon. A pungent mixture of olive oil, vinegar, eggs and mustard, this became known as mayonnaise.

Menorquí even retained a few words of English. So, when British tourists return from a trip to Es Castell (where one may still see Scottish country dancing), they can sit in their hotel dining room, sipping a local gin and contemplating the view through a *boinder* (bow window) until interrupted by a waiter asking if they would like their main course with *grevi*.

✳ THE FOURTEENTH COLONY ✳

Throughout America's war for independence one future state remained loyal to King George III. A stronghold of royalists, it served as a base for operations against the American rebels and fought on tenaciously against vastly superior enemy forces until finally abandoned by the home government after 20 years of dogged efforts to turn it into an imperial asset.

In 1783 St Augustine reverted to being the northernmost outpost of Spain's colonial empire. The city became part of the United States in 1821. The Castillo de San Marcos, built in 1672, is the oldest fort still standing in the US.

If more resources had been committed to its defence or if it had simply been retained and reinforced when the fighting ended, there might have been a very different future for Florida

SPANISH ORIGINS

America's oldest European city, St Augustine, was founded by the Spanish in 1565 to assert control of Florida. Later the Spanish agreed to exchange Florida for Havana (which Britain had seized during the Seven Years War). By then the Spaniards had also founded Pensacola and French colonists had founded Mobile. Both became British.

The Spanish evacuation of Florida was virtually total, leaving the new owners to make a fresh start. The region was divided in two at the line of the Apalachicola River. East Florida, consisting of the peninsula, had its capital at St Augustine. West Florida embraced the Florida panhandle westwards almost to French New Orleans, taking in the coasts of modern Mississippi, Alabama and part of Louisiana. Pensacola became its capital. At Mobile the French accepted alien rule.

The first governor of West Florida, George Johnstone, described Pensacola as 'an assembly of poor despicable huts to the number of 112' but also noted optimistically that it had 'good water, a noble port, beautiful situations surrounding it, infinite communications by water, capable of easy communications by land, great plenty of fish and excellent vegetation'.

Johnstone's successor, Frederick Haldiman, proved most energetic, laying out streets, draining swamps, improving the water supply, building a hospital and a signal house and driving a road through to

Founded by the Spanish in 1559, Pensacola was abandoned in 1661 and reoccupied in 1698. Also variously under French, British, US and Confederate control, this landlocked deepwater port celebrates an annual Fiesta of Five Flags to reflect its chequered history.

Mobile. Under Haldiman the colony's population of soldiers, settlers and slaves trebled to 7,000, and plantations were established to grow indigo, tobacco and citrus. Native Americans traded deerskins and furs for muskets, pots, knives, axes and rum, while the colony also supplied such valued naval stores as timber, tar and turpentine.

A DIFFERENT MODEL

While West Florida hauled itself up by its own efforts, the development of East Florida was supported by the East Florida Society of London, whose members got government grants of 10,000 or 20,000 acres. One member, former doctor Andrew Turnbull, got 40,000 acres for the most ambitious attempt ever at a new settlement in British-controlled America.

In 1767 Turnbull scoured the Mediterranean for would-be settlers, including Greeks, Cretans, Sicilians, Italians and Corsicans – not quite what the British authorities had in mind when specifying his settlers should be 'white Protestants'.

The largest single contingent in Turnbull's trawl was recruited from Minorca and the group collectively became known as Minorcans. In 1768 1,400 settlers established 'New Smyrna', named in honour of the birthplace of Turnbull's Greek wife.

Encouraged by Turnbull's initiative, Francis Levett established a 10,000-acre plantation, overlooking the St John's River, which he named Julianton in honour of his wife. Here he built a 14-room mansion, plus 50 farm buildings, a 180-foot wharf and a formal English garden, two riverfront 'hanging gardens', a peach orchard, orange groves and a vineyard with 3,000 vines.

LOYALIST STRONGHOLD

The outbreak of the American revolutionary war in 1775 boosted the Floridas as reinforcements arrived for their defence and loyalists from Georgia and the Carolinas fled there as a royalist haven.

Apart from regular infantry, there were German units, loyalists from Pennsylvania and Maryland, and volunteer militia units – the South Carolina Royalists, the Royal North Carolina Regiment, the St Augustine Grenadiers and the East Florida Rangers. Unlike the American rebels, the Rangers included black fighters, whereas the 'patriots', struggling for freedom, would not trust them with weapons.

In 1777 a force from Florida, consisting of regulars, local 'rangers' and Creek Indians, marched into Georgia, captured and burned Fort McIntosh and returned with 2,000 head of cattle as booty. In 1778 contingents from Florida converged with a force from New York to capture the important port of Savannah.

Three successive rebel invasion attempts from Georgia failed.

But there were also adverse developments unconnected with the war. In 1777 the settlers of New Smyrna, reduced by two-thirds by disease and raids by hostile Native Americans, deserted to St Augustine. In 1778 West Florida was devastated by a hurricane.

When Spain decided to join France on the side of the American rebels, Florida was doomed. Nevertheless, St Augustine held out until the ending of hostilities, when its defenders were appalled to learn that the two Floridas were to be handed back to Spain.

AFTERMATH

Of Florida's loyalist population of 17,000 only 1,000 chose to remain.

Some returned to the now independent United States to reclaim abandoned properties.

Others moved west to settle along the Mississippi, under French rule.

Most scattered through the empire, from Nova Scotia to the Bahamas, from London to Sierra Leone.

Julianton was deserted by its owners, a prize plum for some lucky Spaniard.

LEGACY OF EMPIRE

Strange to say, a legacy lingers. At St Augustine there is a winter British Night Watch Parade in which enthusiastic re-enactors, dressed in the uniforms of the Sixtieth Regiment and the East Florida Rangers, march to fife and drum and perform a traditional changing of the guard ceremony.

At Pensacola, Holy Trinity Episcopalian church mounts a summer British Festival featuring tea, fish and chips and Scotch eggs to the accompaniment of the kilted pipe band from McGuire's Irish Pub.

Pensacola's other annual celebrations include gatherings of devotees of British cars and British motorcycles.

Finally there is the Dominion of British West Florida, which has its own flag and has issued currency in honour of the eightieth birthday of HM Queen Elizabeth II. Claiming that the British cession of the Floridas in 1783 was technically flawed in international law, the would-be Dominion has petitioned Her Majesty for readmission to British Sovereignty.

✷ THE OTHER UNITED STATES ✷

In this United States they played cricket, took afternoon tea and spoke Greek – or Italian. Except for the people who ran it, who often didn't bother to speak either language and wanted to keep their distance from a local populace notable for 'the constant use of garlic and the rare use of soap'.

The United States of the Ionian Islands lasted for half a century and for a century after that its former citizens continued to use yards and pints. Now only the cricket remains.

FOREIGN MASTERS

Originally colonized by Corinth, the Ionian Islands were then ruled by Macedonians, Romans, Byzantines and Venetians but, importantly

THE ARCHIPELAGO

The seven islands of the Ionian archipelago lie off the northwestern coast of Greece:

The largest is Cephalonia, the setting for Louis de Bernieres' best-selling novel, *Captain Corelli's Mandolin*.

The second largest is Corfu, whose fate triggered the Peloponnesian War, which destroyed both Athens and Sparta.

Lawrence Durrell's well-known travel book *Prospero's Cell* (1945) was based on his pre-war years at Kalami on Corfu.

Ithaca was supposedly the home of Odysseus, but the geography doesn't quite fit. Lord Byron still thought he might quite like to buy it.

Levkas is supposedly where lovesick Sappho died.

Zakynthos was the birthplace of the Italian poet and patriot Ugo Foscolo.

The other islands of the group, Paxos and Kythira, are vaguely familiar to modern Britons as holiday destinations.

and uniquely for Greeks, never by the Ottomans, which kept the islands just that little bit more Greek. Briefly annexed by revolutionary France, the islands then had seven years of virtual independence as the Septinsular Republic.

A PROTECTING POWER

Between 1809 and 1814 the archipelago was taken by the British, who persuaded the other European powers that a new entity – the United States of the Ionian Islands – would be best served by British 'protection'. The islanders got a constitution with an advisory assembly whose advice could be ignored and a Lord High Commissioner who had all the real power.

The Ionians also got their own flag, with a Union Jack in one corner and the winged Lion of St Mark of Venice in another, and a very handsome coinage to go with it.

EXPORTING ENGLISHNESS

For the Ionians, foreign rule brought schools and hospitals and the best-surfaced and densest road network in all Greece, as well as a bank and a postal system, lighthouses, lock-ups, lunatic asylums and courts that couldn't be bribed.

Some of the innovations were very alien priorities, like improved sanitation; the local term 'English house' meant one with a bathroom. Ditto the bandstand and the botanic garden. The potato was introduced to local cultivation and apple chutney to the local dining table.

Lasting legacy – cricket on Corfu. Victorian gentlemen contend at a leisurely pace before onlookers wearing British fashions and Corfiote costume. The mighty fortress in the background underlines British strategic interest in the island and its neighbours.

LORDS OF THE ISLES

Effectively wielding entirely individual power, British rulers of the Ionian Islands were free to make a personal mark.

'KING TOM'

The first Lord High Commissioner, hard-drinking, loud-mouthed, despotic 'King Tom' Maitland, laid out an esplanade and imported Maltese stone and Maltese masons to build two imposing palaces, one in Corfu and one as a seaside retreat. It was in the latter of these that the Duke of Edinburgh, future husband of Elizabeth II, would be born.

GOING GREEK

Maitland's successor, Sir Frederick Adam, founded a university whose chancellor was the Earl of Guilford. The earl spoke the local dialect of Greek fluently and wrote posh Greek beautifully. He was also a convert to the Greek Orthodox Church and habitually dressed in ancient Greek costume.

LOCAL HERO

Cephalonia, in particular, benefited from the energy of the young Charles Napier, who learned both Greek and Italian and rushed around building things. Byron thought so highly of Napier that on his deathbed he nominated him to command the Greek revolt against Ottoman rule. The Cephalonians returned Napier's regard and there are public gardens named after him.

Tourism developed, attracting the whimsical poet and painter Edward Lear and a youthful Disraeli, tracing the footsteps of his idol Byron, with Byron's own valet in tow.

BADGE OF HONOUR

The occupiers thought their rule would be strengthened by co-opting the cooperative. In 1818, therefore, the Prince Regent established the Order of St Michael and St George, for meritorious service to the Crown by inhabitants or officials of the Ionian Islands and Malta. Recipients were given a badge of impressive splendour, bearing the optimistic motto *Auspicium melioris aevi* (Sign of a Better Age).

OBJECTIONABLE OTTO

Once mainland Greece achieved full independence in 1830, the Ionians wanted *enosis* – union – with their compatriots. The Royal Navy thought otherwise, considering the islands essential for control of the eastern Mediterranean.

Besides which, the King of Greece, Otto I, was pro-German – scarcely surprising as he was born a Bavarian prince. As a Catholic in an Orthodox country he was never ideal for the Greek throne.

During the Crimean War, while Britain and France fought to protect the ramshackle Ottoman Empire from Russia, Otto decided to side with the Russians, provoking the British and French to occupy the port of Athens – thus rather making the Royal Navy's point.

AN ACCEPTABLE ALLY

The Greeks finally sent Otto back to Bavaria in 1862 and replaced him with a Dane, called William, who called himself George I. His sister, Alexandra, married the Prince of Wales, putting George firmly in the British camp.

In 1864 Britain therefore returned the United States of the Ionian Islands to Greece – after blowing up the fortifications, just in case....

George I reigned for 50 years, founding a dynasty that lasted as long as the monarchy did. Britain meanwhile enlarged the scope of the Order of St Michael and St George to award it for foreign service *not* necessarily connected with the Ionian Islands and Malta.

SOURCES OF ILLUSTRATIONS

a=above; c=centre; b=below

1 Wynkyn de Worde, *Introductio Lingue Latine*, 1495. Master & Fellows of Magdalene College, Cambridge. 2 Anon., *Henry, Earl of Richmond at the Battle of Bosworth Field*, c. 1840. 4a Diagram of a windmill, from W. Blith's *The English Improver Improved*, 1652. 4b J. Fairburn, *British Sailors Boarding an Algerian Pirate Ship*, 18th century. National Maritime Museum, London. 5 Coat of arms of the Bedford Level Corporation, from Jonas Moore's map of 1706. 7 Detail from *William Bruges, first Garter Knight of Arms before St George*. British Library, London. 9 Illustrations from John Speed's *Historie of Great Britaine*, 1611. 12 The Departure of the Romans, 14th century. British Library, London. 15 Sketches of Cadbury-Camelot from William Musgrave's *Antiquitates Britanno-Belgicae*, 1719. 21 Reconstruction of helmet from Sutton Hoo. British Museum, London. 24 The Venerable Bede, 12th century. British Library, London. 25 Initium of St Mark's Gospel, The Lindisfarne Gospels, 7–8th century. British Library, London. 29 The Alfred Jewel, 9th century. Ashmolean Museum, Oxford. 47 Paul Sandby, *Nuneham House*, 18th century. Private Collection/ Bridgeman Art Library. 54 'Fen Slodgers' from P. Thompson's *History and Antiquities of Boston*, 1856. 60 *A Ship of the Short Blue Fleet*, 1864. London Borough of Barking and Dagenham. 71 *An English Celebration of the Defeat of the Spanish Armada*. British Museum, London.

77 Inigo Jones, *A Watery Spirit in the Temple of Love*, early 17th century. Devonshire Collection, Chatsworth, Derbyshire. 79 *William and Mary in London*, 17th century. British Museum, London. 83 attr. Theodore Lane, *The Long and the Short of the Tale*, 1821. National Portrait Gallery, London. 87 Anon., *A Correct Plan and Elevation of the Famous French Raft Constructed for the Invasion of England*, 18th century. British Museum, London. 88 Richard Caton Woodville, *Battle of Towton*, 1461. Illustration from Hutchinson's *Story of the British Nation*, 1920s. Bridgeman Art Library. 91 Samuel Pepys's endplate. Master & Fellows of Magdalene College, Cambridge. 92 Robert Hooke, A flea and a louse from *The Micrographia*, 1665. 94 *Regency Dandies*, 19th century. Museum of London. 98 Regent's Quadrant from Elmes's *Metropolitan Improvements*, 1827. 101 Suffragettes in Trafalgar Square, *Punch*, 1911. 104 *Red Lion Square*, 1800. Mary Evans Picture Library. 106 Francesco Bartolozzi, illustration from John Howard's *The State of English & Foreign Prisons*, 1780. 109 John Calcott, The first Christmas card for Sir Henry Cole, 1843. Victoria & Albert Museum, London. 111 Illustrations from Domenico Angelo's *L'École des armes*, 1763. 120 Anon., *Mrs Delaney*. British Museum, London. 122 'Comment on Poverty', *Punch*, vol. XV, 1848. 130 Illustration from John Dennys's *The Secrets of Angling*, 1652. 133 *Jonathan's Coffee House*, 1763. British Museum, London. 134 Illustration from

Hannah Glasse's *Art of Cookery*, 1750s. Wellcome Library, London. **140-41** *The Kitchen Department of the Reform Club* from Alexis Soyer's *The Gastronomic Regenerator*, 1846. **144** 'Entombment of St Edmund at Bury' from John Lydgate's *The Lives of Sts Edmund & Fredmund*, 15th century. British Library, London. **147** *The Cruell Burning of Five Martyrs in Smithfield, April 12 1557* from John Foxe's *The Book of Martyrs*. British Museum, London. **150** Illustration from *The Famous History of the Lancashire Witches*, 18th century. **156** 'Fleet Marriage' from Robert Chambers's *The Book of Days*, 1869. **161** After William Henry Pickersgill, *Hannah More*, 18th century. Bridgeman Art Library, London. **169** After Charles Furse, *Field Marshal Lord Roberts on his Arab Charger Volonel*, 20th century. **173** Philip Morgan, *A Prospect of Tangier from the Westward after it was Demolished*, c. 1683. The Master and Fellows of Magdalene College, Cambridge. **175** Anon., *The Shooting of Admiral Byng on Board the Monarque*, 1757. **177** Baptista Boazio, Map depicting the destruction of the Spanish Colony of St Augustine, Florida, 16th century. Private Collection/Bridgeman Art Library, London. **178** *A View of Pensacola in West Florida* published by George Gauld, c. 1775. Library of Congress Prints & Photographs Division, Washington DC. **183** 'Cricket on Corfu' from *The Illustrated London News*, 1853. Mary Evans Picture Library, London.

SOURCES OF QUOTATIONS

p. 13: J. N. L. Myres, *The English Settlements*, 1986; p. 34: G. M. Trevelyan, *Clio: A Muse*, 1913; p. 100: A. J. P. Taylor, *English History 1914-45*, 1970; p. 134: G. B. Shaw, *Man & Superman*, 1903.

INDEX

Page numbers in *italics* indicate illustrations.

Accum, Friedrich 136–7
Acre 8
Adrian IV, Pope 145
advertising 90
Aethelred II, 'the Unready' 28, 32
Africa 119, 165, 167
Agricola 11
Albert, Prince Consort 69, 109
Alcock, Charles 114–5
aldermen 8
Alfred the Great, King 26–9, 30, 31, 33
Alfred Jewel 29, *29*
America, Americans 8, 33, 58, 59, 62–3, 81, 87, 92, 114, 121, 124, 126, 132, 135, 138, 139, 149, 153, 176–81; *see also* Florida
'Ancient Britons' 9, *9*
Angelo, Domenico 111, *111*, 116
Anglo-Saxons 8, 9, 11, 12, *12*, 13, 19–32, 35, 37, 38–40
Anglo-Saxon Chronicle 27, 28, 38, 40
Anne, Queen 69
Anne of Denmark 69, 76
Arabs, Arabic 35, 108, 118
archaeology 15, 19, 21, 35, 37, 43–9, 57–8, 88, 90
Archer, Fred 115
Armada, Spanish 70–71, *71*, 74

Army, British 91, 92–3, 97, 117, 139–41
Arne, Thomas 80
Arthur, King 8, 13–19, *16*, 76
Ashmolean Museum 29
Athelstan 30
Austen, Jane 94, 119, 160
Australia, Australians 6, 95, 117, 120

Banting, William 138–9
Barbon, Dr Nicholas 103–4
Barclay, Captain 113
Barking 22, 60–61, *60*
Bath 14, 27, 31, 107–8, *108*, 112, 131, 160
battles 10, 13, 14, 19, 21, 23, 27, 84–9, *88*, 92; Battle of Maldon 21
Bayeux Tapestry 38–9, *39*
Beckford, William 107–8, *108*
Bede, Venerable 23–4, *24*, 28, 29, 33, 144
Beeton, Mrs Isabella 141–2
Behan, Aphra 119
Bergman-Osterberg, Madame 124
Berkshire 48, 96
Bible 15, 81
billiards 114, 116, 118
Birkenhead, HMS 99
Black Death 36, 44, 46, 49, 128
Blakeney, William 175
Boer War 124, 168, 169
Bonnie Prince Charlie 80

boxers, boxing 64, 83, 97, 112–13
Breakspear, Nicholas 145
Britannia 9, 11, 12, 19
Brittany 14, 68
Burdett-Coutts, Angela 120–1, *121*
Burgoyne, Field Marshal Sir John Fox 167
Burgundians, Burgundy 36, 70, 88–9
burhs 27, 38
burials 19, 21, 45, 117, 163; *see also* Westminster Abbey
Butler, Josephine 121–2
Byng, Admiral John 174–5, *175*
Byron, Lord George Gordon 98, 111, 182, 184

Cadiz 93, 170
Caesar, Julius 9, 10
Camberwell 107, 162
Cambridge 28, 50–53, 57, 68, 72, 105, 131, 148
Camden, William 42, 53, 54, 55
Camelot 15, *15*, 16, 19
Campbell, Sir Colin 167, 168
Canterbury 28
Caroline, Princess 82–3, *83*
castles 38–9
cathedrals 39–40
Catholic, Roman 70–1, 78–9, 95, 129–30, 146–51, 157, 185

Caxton, William 18
Cephalonia 182, 184
Charles I, King 69, 76, 77, 149
Charles II, King 6, 57, 69, 91, 131, 170, 172
Chavasse, Noel and Christopher 125–6
Chelsea Hospital 99, 169
Christianity 7, 12, *16*, 21, 23–6, 27, 29, 31, 32–3, 39, 70–1, 73, 78–9, 91, 105, 124–5, 143–62, 179; *see also* different denominations
Christmas 15, 109, *109*, 145, 149, *149*
Churchill, Sir Winston 17
Civil Wars 86, 89–92, 149
Claudius 10
coffee houses 130–33, *133*, 169
coins, coinage 29, 30, 35, *35*, 73
Cole, Henry 109
Colchester 10, 15, 92
Corfu 182, *183*, 184, 185
Cornwall 14, 15, 16, 41, 44, 144
coronation 31–2, 70, 72, 79, *79*, 83
cricket 96–7, 113, 114, 115, 118, 181, *183*
Crimean War 140–41, 165, 66, 167, 185
Cumbria 14, 128
Cuthbert, St 24–5

Dartmoor 41, 43, 44, 95
Dee, Dr John 72
Defoe, Daniel 50, 51, 52, 54, 60

Delany, Mrs 120, *120*
Denmark, Danes 19, 29, 30, 31, 69, 76, 185
deserted villages 43–9
Devon 27, 41, 49, 79, 128
Dod, Charlotte 'Lottie' 115–16, *115*
Domesday Book 36, 39, 40, 41
Dorset 14, 27, 39, 48
Dublin 140, 175
Dunstan, St 31, 32
Dunwich 36
Durham Cathedral 25, 26
Dutch 9, 55, 69, 78–9, 119

East Anglia 21, 35, 36, 144, 148, 153
East India Company 58, 90
Ecgfrith 35
Edgar 30–32
Edinburgh 14, 98, 107, 125
Edmund 'the Elder' 30
Edmund, St 41, 144, *144*
Edred 30
Edward 'the Confessor' 28
Edward 'the Elder' 30
Edward 'the Martyr' 32
Edward I, King 15, 17, 36, 66, 129
Edward III, King 17, 33
Edward IV, King 85–6
Edward VII, King 70
Egypt 11, 65, 96, 165
Elizabeth I, Queen 57, 68, 72–5, 130, 147
Elizabeth II, Queen 181
Elliott, Launceston 117
emigration 122–3, *122*, 140
English language 21, 25, 26, 28, 65–9, 96, 134–5, 138, 146

Essex 10, 15, 21, 35, 40, 41, 44, 58–9, 105, 151–2, 153
Essex, Robert Devereux, Earl of 74–5
Eton 97, 111
Excalibur 13, 16, 18
Exeter 11, 79, 153

famine 40, 76, 120, 127–8, 140, 168
fasting and dieting 115, 129–30, 138–9
Fens, The 53–5, *54*, 128
First World War 100–102, 116, 125, 126, 160
fish and fishing 36, 44, 49, 60–61, *60*, 129–30, *130*, 178
Fleet Weddings 155–6, *156*
Flemings 9, 11
Florida 176–81
food 97, 102, 127–42, *134*, *137*, 174, 176
Forest Law 40–42
Forest of Dean 41, 42
Foxe, John 146–7; *Book of Martyrs* 146–7, *147*
France, French 14, 16, 58, 62, 67, 68, 69, 70, 71, 78, 81, 87, 90, 94, 105, 108, 113, 118, 122, 133, 136, 138, 139–41, 145, 149, 161, 172, 174–6, 180, 181, 185
Frere, Sir Bartle 165
Froissart, Jean 17
Fry, C. B. 118–19

gardens, gardening 47, *47*, 56, 57, 58, 59, 95, 102
Gaul, Gauls 10, 24
Genoa 33, 73
Geoffrey of Monmouth 13, 14, 15, 16

George I, King 69

George II, King 69, 80

George III, King 58, 69, 82, 95, 111, 176

George IV (Prince Regent) 82–3, 111, 184

George V, King 116

George, St 7, 32–3

Germany, Germans 9, 11, 19, 26, 67, 68, 69, 78, 81, 82–3, 96, 100, 116–17, 136–7, 138, 164, 180, 185

Gibraltar 174

Gildas 13, 14, 19

Glasse, Hannah 133–5, *134*

Glastonbury 14, 16, 17

Gloucester, Gloucestershire 11, 44, 49, 144

golf 59, 115

Gordon, General Charles 166, *166*, 167, 168

Granby, Marquis of, John Manners 92–3

Grant, Baron Albert 110

Great Exhibition 109, 140, 168

Greece, Greeks 9, 11, 33, 67–9, 117, 179, 181–5

Greenwich 71

Gresham, Sir Thomas 73

Gresham College 73, 89

Hadrian's Wall 10, 34, 36

Hampshire 15, 20, 41, 118

Hardwicke, Lord 156–7

Harrow 97, 114

'Harrying of the North' 40

Hatton, Sir Christopher 72–3

Havelock, General Sir Henry 6, 164, *164*, 169

Henry I, King 66

Henry II, King 41, 87, 145

Henry III, King 41, 66

Henry IV, King 67

Henry V, King 67

Henry VI, King 84–6

Henry VII, King 2, 18, 68, 87

Henry VIII, King 15, 26, 46, 55–7, 68

Hereward the Wake 55

Hertfordshire 41, 43

Hill, Octavia 122–3

Hooke, Robert 92, *92*

Hopkins, Matthew 153

hospitals 36, 50, 97, 100

housing 120, 122–3

Howard, John 105

Huguenots 9

Hunsdon, Baron Henry Carey 74

hunting 40–42, 55–7

Huntingdon, Henry of 8

India 163–5, 166–70

invasions 9, 10, 19–20, 38, 78–9, 87, 145

Ionian Islands 181–5, *183*; *see also* individual islands

Ireland, Irish 7, 9, 10, 62, 70, 95, 111, 127, 140, 145, 151, 167, 171, 175, 181

Isle of Wight 20, 44, 87

Italy, Italians 9, 56, 62, 67, 68, 70, 73–5, *83*, 90, 110, 111, 113, 118, 122, 125, 132, 151, 179, 181, 182, 184

James VI (and I), King 69, 76

James VII (and II), King 69, 78–9

Jews 9, 74–5, 112–13, 131, 157

John, King 41, 50

Jones, Inigo 75–7

Jonson, Ben 75

Julianton 179, 180

Jutes 20

Kent 10, 20, 29, 35, 41, 107, 119

Kingston-on-Thames 31, 32

Kipling, Rudyard 12, 19, 34, 38, 65, 163

Kiralfy, Imre 62–3

Latin 1, 9, 11, 12, 28, 29, 66, 67, 68, 69, 146, 155, 163

law, laws 8, 20, 22, 29, 30, 40–42, 46, 98, 121–2, 138, 143, 151, 160

Leicester, Robert Dudley, Earl of 74

Leicester, Leicestershire 11, 30, 46, 51, 92

Lettsom, Dr John Coakley 106–107

Lichfield 35

Lincoln, Lincolnshire 14, 30, 45

Lindisfarne Gospels 7, 24–5, *25*

Liverpool 121, 125

London 27, 32, 41, 51, 60, 62–4, *63*, 73, 79, *79*, 80, 85, 89, 90, 92, 103–104, *104*, 107, 110, 123, 124, 128, 131–3, *133*, 136, 148, *164*, 179; *see also* individual monuments, buildings and districts

Lopez, Dr Rodrigo 74–5

Magna Carta 42, 108, 144
Malory, Sir Thomas 15, 18
Malta 105, 184, 185
Manchester 11, 37
marathon 64
marriage 70-71,
    154-60, *156*
Mary I, Queen 57, 70-71,
    73, 146, 155
Mary II, Queen 69,
    78-9, *79*
Mary, Queen of Scots 72
masques 75-8, *77*
mayonnaise 176
Medway, River 20, 119
Mendoza, Daniel 112-13,
    112
Mercia 29, 30, 35, 37
milk 129, 135-6
Minorca 174-6, 179
monasteries 16, 17, 23-4,
    25-6, 28-9, 31, 36, 39,
    45, 56, 152
More, Hannah 160-62
More, Sir Thomas 45
Morocco 170-73, *173*
Mount Badon, battle of
    13, 14
Mussabini, 'Sam' 118

Napier, General Charles
    163-4, 169, 184
Napoleonic Wars 94-8
national anthems 80-81
Netherlands 19, 26, 69, 73,
    78, 105, 113, 122
New Forest 41, 42
New Smyrna 179-80
New Zealand 6, 164
Nightingale, Florence
    140, 141
Nonsuch 46, 55-8, *56*

Norfolk 39, 43, 46, 49, 61,
    92, 144
Normans 8, 9, 21, 38-43,
    39, 55, 65, 66
Northamptonshire 43, 45,
    73, 84
Northumbria 23-6, 30
Norwich 22, 50
Nuneham Courtney
    46-8, *47*

Offa's Dyke 35, 37
Offa the Great 35, *35*, 37,
    144
Olympic Games 62-4, 115,
    117, 118, 125, 126
Order of the Garter 17, 33,
    73, 74
Order of St Michael and
    St George 184, 185
Osbaldestone, Squire
    113-14
Outram, Sir James 165,
    165, 169
Oxford, Oxfordshire 13,
    27-9, 32, 45-8, *47*, 66, 68,
    73, 89, 90, 118, 124, 125,
    131, 146, 162

Palavicino, Sir Horatio
    73-4
Paris 67, 72, 90, 108, 111
parks 42, 46-8
Parliament 18, 36, 66, 70,
    73, 77-9, 83, 91, 92, 105;
    Acts of 46, 66, 80, 98,
    121-2, 138, 149, 159
Pasteur, Louis 136, 138
penny 8, 35
Pensacola 177-8, *178*
Pepys, Samuel 91, *91*,
    170, 172

Philip II, King of Spain
    70-71, 75
physical education 124
plague 20, 44, 45, 128, 147
Poland, Polish 68, 72
Popes 26, 39, 65, 143-5,
    150, 151, 154; *see also*
    names of individual
    Popes
population 20, 40, 43-9,
    97, 127-8
Portugal, Portuguese 33,
    69, 74-5, 170-72
prisons, prisoners 22, 95,
    105-106, *106*, 109
prostitutes, prostitution
    53, 120, 121-2, 172
Prynne, William 77
Puritans 76, 77, 91, 131,
    147-50, *149*
Pytheas of Marseilles 9

Quakers 91, 106-7, 157

rabbits 43
Ray, John 43
Red Lion Square 104, *104*
Reform Club 139, *141*
Regent Street 97, *98*
Richard I, King 66
Richard II, King 66
roads, road transport 12,
    90, 128, 165, 183
Roberts, Field Marshal
    Frederick Sleigh 168-9,
    169
Romans 8, 9, 10-12, *12*, 14,
    19, 27, 29, 32-3, 36, 38, 55,
    144, 181
Rome 12, 39, 62, 143-5
Round Table 14-17
Royal Air Force 126

INDEX

Royal Exchange 73, 104, 156
Royal Navy 4, 26, 27, 81, 91, 93, 97, 99, 119, 124, 130, 170–76, 175, 184–5
Royal Society 89, 92, 120
Russia, Russians 33, 78, 106, 165, 166, 185

St Albans 85, 144, 145
St Augustine (city) 177, 177, 180
St Paul's Cathedral 6, 73, 105, 126
saints 143–4; see also names of individual saints
Sandow, Eugene 116–17
Scotland, Scots 7, 10, 14, 30, 61, 67–9, 72, 76, 80, 86, 99, 114, 125, 149, 151, 171
Second World War 34, 48–9, 102
Shaftesbury 27
Shakespeare 67, 75, 84, 98
sheep 42, 45–6, 94, 142
slavery 11, 94, 98, 107, 119, 143, 161, 165, 172, 178, 179
Smollett, Tobias 135–6
Soho 104, 111, 138
Somerset 27, 29, 41
South Africa, South Africans 99, 118, 120, 124, 168, 169
Southampton 22, 87, 119
Southwark 75
Soyer, Alexis 139–41
Spain, Spanish 33, 43, 68, 70–71, 74, 76, 81, 93, 94–5, 151, 163, 174–7, 180
sport 62–4, 91, 96–7, 111–19, 124, 125

Spurgeon, Charles Haddon 162
Staffordshire 91, 92, 128
Stamford 27, 30, 50
Stephen, King 28, 87
Stourbridge Fair 50–53
Suetonius 10
Suffolk 36, 144
Suffragettes 101
Sussex 34, 35, 41, 118, 126, 151
Sutton Hoo 20–21, 21
Sweden, Swedish 58, 62, 124, 138
Switzerland, Swiss 95, 122, 151, 178

Tacitus 11
Tangier 6, 170–73, 173
tennis 113, 115
theatre 75–8, 160
Tintagel 15
Tower of London 77, 168
Towton, Battle of 84–6, 88–9, 88
Trafalgar Square 6, 163–4, 164
Tyneham 48–9

Union Jack 7
Upton 43–4

Venice 72, 181, 182
Victoria, Queen 69, 121, 165, 169
Victoria Cross 126, 168, 170
Vikings 9, 25–30
Volonel 168–9, 168
Voltaire 127, 175

Wade, Field Marshal 80–81
Wakley, Dr Thomas 137–8

Wales, Welsh 7, 10, 13, 14, 15, 17, 18, 22, 30, 35, 37, 68, 69, 76, 87, 96
Wanstead House 58–9, 59
Ward, Mrs Humphry 124–5
Wars of the Roses 84–9
Warwickshire 18, 43
Washington, George 59
Wellington, Duke of 59, 163
Wesley, John 162
Wessex 26–31
Westminster Abbey 74, 165, 175
Wharram Percy 43, 44
White, Field Marshal Sir George 170
White, T. H. 18
White City 62–4, 63
William I, 'the Conqueror' 38–40, 55, 66
William III, King 69, 78–9, 79
William of Malmesbury 16, 39, 40, 41, 66
Wiltshire 14, 48, 108
Wimbledon 115
Winchester 11, 15, 26, 27, 28, 70, 144
Windsor 17, 64, 82, 100
Wisden, John 114
witches, witchcraft 69, 150–53, 150
Wolseley, Viscount General Garnet 166–8, 168
Worde, Wynkyn, de 1

York 23, 26, 30, 31, 85
Yorkshire 15, 40, 41, 44, 46, 49, 84–6, 88–9, 92, 171